Get the Self-Esteem Habit

Get the Self-Esteem Habit

How You Can Choose to Have Confidence and Succeed in Life

Christine Webber

HELP YOURSELF

First published in Great Britain in 2002

10 9 8 7 6 5 4 3 2 1

British Library Cataloguing in Publication Data
A record for this book is available from the British Library

ISBN 0 340 78650 7

Typeset by Avon Dataset Ltd, Bidford-on-Avon, Warks

Printed and bound in Great Britain by
Bookmarque

Hodder & Stoughton
A Division of Hodder Headline Ltd
338 Euston Road
London NW1 3BH
www.madaboutbooks.com

To my darling David,
with heartfelt thanks for all the love and laughter.

Contents

Acknowledgements

I am so grateful to Judith Longman at Hodder. Thanks, Judith. It's such a pleasure to be doing another book with you.

I would also like to thank my agent Ali Gunn at Curtis Brown for being marvellously supportive, very perceptive – and great fun at all times.

I'm also grateful to my very special niece, Alex Webber, for all her help with my research.

And, finally, a big thank you to all the people I've talked to while preparing *Get the Self-Esteem Habit*. Many of your details have been altered to protect your confidentiality – but you know who you are.

1

What is Self-Esteem? What's Yours Like? How Can You Get a Good Self-Esteem Habit?

Introduction

Who's your favourite person? Is it you? If not, I hope I can persuade you to *become* your favourite person by the end of the book.

After all, you're with yourself twenty-four hours a day. You also know yourself better than you know anyone else – even if you don't always understand your behaviour. And you're in a unique position to mould yourself into the individual you want to be. In fact, you're the *only* person in life you can guarantee to change. And you can become someone whom you really, really like.

But, in order to become your own favourite person, you need to:

- like yourself;
- value yourself;
- care for yourself;
- accept yourself.

And none of this is easy if you don't have much self-esteem.

So, what *is* self-esteem, exactly? It's a term everyone uses, but it's not that easy to define. Some people think it's about feeling confident and happy – which it is, but it's more than that. It's actually a measurement of how we perceive ourselves: an estimation, or a rating, of our worth.

Unfortunately, plenty of adults – very nice, decent, sensitive, kind, generous, loving adults at that – don't give themselves anything like a good enough rating. And this tendency to undervalue themselves can make their life hell.

Is this ringing any bells with you? I imagine it is – or you wouldn't have gone to the trouble of buying this book.

Poor self-esteem is at the root of all sorts of problems. Clearly, it prevents us from feeling wonderfully contented, or from having peace of mind. It can also contribute to depression, insomnia, stress, isolation and loneliness.

At its most extreme it also causes addictive behaviour, domestic violence and petty crime. And it therefore follows that if more people had good self-esteem, there would be fewer drug addicts and alcoholics, fewer violent relationships, fewer crowded jails – and millions and millions of happier people in the world.

So having healthy self-esteem is great. But is it possible to acquire it if you don't have it?

The answer is a resounding 'yes'. In fact, you can work on developing it till it becomes a habit.

Taking up a good habit – like going to the gym, or eating more healthily – can feel just as hard, initially, as eradicating a bad one like smoking. And it's possible that you're afraid you'll fail. Maybe you're even thinking: well, it's easy for her to write this stuff, but I'm the one who's going to have to develop this habit – and I bet it's really hard.

OK, it *is* hard. But it's *not* impossible, and that's why I'm urging you to commit to doing it – because once you value yourself more, everything about your life will start to improve.

Developing a good self-esteem habit is all about *change* – and change is never simple. Changing relationships, changing jobs, moving house . . . all these things are problematic, but we get through them. And, usually, when we look back, we're very pleased that we made the *effort* to change.

Good changes are almost always an effort – and changing yourself from someone who has poor self-esteem into someone who has healthy self-esteem is no exception. But you'll be delighted you did it, even though it won't happen overnight.

Suppose, for a moment, that you'd been playing tennis with your sister down at the park since you were a child. You'd never had any lessons, and you didn't really know what you were doing, but you struggled on. However, one day, while you were idly watching Wimbledon on the television, you suddenly realised just how many bad habits you had, and you decided that you'd love to learn to play better. So, you signed up for some coaching.

At the first session, the coach told you you were holding your racquet the wrong way and that you weren't keeping your eye on the ball. He encouraged you to alter those things. Easier said than done! Everything he suggested felt very awkward and you got more and more fed up. You started swearing under your breath and kept sneaking a look at your watch, longing for the hour to be over. In fact, you made a pact with yourself that as soon as the lesson was finished, you'd go back to your old ways and never try to change again.

But then, all of sudden, what the coach was telling you began to make sense. You were amazed to hear a new sound when your racquet struck the ball and you could feel and see that you were hitting it harder and more accurately. Your mood changed. You started smiling. Perhaps this new advice was worth persevering with after all . . .

How long do you think it would take to eradicate the bad habits which had taken some twenty years to build up and to replace them with good ones?

Hopefully, it wouldn't take *another* twenty years or so, but I think you'd agree that it wouldn't happen instantly.

However, over the next few weeks – with practice and help – you'd find that you were striking the ball more confidently and timing your shots better. And you'd feel proud that you'd spotted you had a problem, and that you'd invested time and energy in sorting it out. You'd probably admit to yourself that you'd never have improved if you'd carried on with all your old, bad habits.

In the same way, cultivating the habit of good self-esteem will also take time and effort, but you'll be giving yourself the gift of a new, more confident and happier life.

In this book, we'll be looking at how you can gain a good self-esteem habit by changing:

- how you think;
- how you feel;
- how you behave;
- how you speak about yourself.

Later in the book, I'll be giving you some hints and tips about changing unhelpful behaviour and speech. But the bulk of the work you're going to tackle will be about changing your thoughts and feelings.

So, let's get going right away on how you think and feel about yourself by establishing some goals you should aim for. Achieving these goals will provide you with the backbone of your new habit of good self-esteem.

Goals

1. Learn to like yourself.
2. Learn to value yourself.
3. Learn to care for yourself.
4. Learn to feel happy in your own skin.
5. Learn to trust and believe in yourself.
6. Learn to respect yourself.
7. Learn to be responsible for yourself.
8. Learn to totally accept yourself – body and soul.

Personal responsibility

The first six of the eight goals listed above may be difficult – but they need no explanation.

However, sometimes people don't understand goals 7 and 8. 'Why do I have to be responsible for myself?' they ask.

The reason is that we are all living longer than ever before, and we're changing jobs and partners more than at any time in history. In this climate of change, the only thing that makes sense is to be appropriately self-reliant. Those who have grasped this fact, and who are in charge – and in control – of their own lives, are those with the greatest self-regard.

If they don't have enough money, they work harder, or do overtime, or embark on further education or training so that they can earn more. Alternatively, they down-size, or re-think their priorities.

If they make a mistake, they admit it. But they don't beat themselves up over it – they resolve to learn from it and do better next time.

If they're in a relationship that demeans them – they pluck up courage to assert themselves within it, or to leave.

Their lives – like everyone else's – have their ups and downs, but they reckon that whatever happens to them is their own business, and their own responsibility.

Of course they can feel highly delighted if some other lovely person comes into their life and augments their good feelings about themselves, offering them love and companionship, and sharing various tasks and responsibilities – but they don't expect this person to take over, and to solve all life's problems for them. And they certainly don't live in a kind of limbo waiting for 'Mr Right' or 'Miss Right' to come along and make everything OK.

Frequently, adults with poor self-esteem try to avoid this kind of responsibility. Instead, they latch on to someone else, such as a confident partner – or even just a friend – in the belief that they'll become more significant in the world's eyes as well as in their own; and that they'll be swept through the mainstream of life in the wake of this other person.

But this isn't the answer to their problems. In fact, when people believe that their happiness or validity is dependent on another individual, they spend their whole time worrying that they're going to be rejected by the other person and end up alone and vulnerable again.

Unfortunately, this anxiety leads them to behave in a very 'clingy' way, which almost guarantees that the worst happens and that the friendship or relationship *does* go wrong. And when it does, poor self-esteem reaches rock bottom.

The only viable alternative is for us to accept that we're in charge of our own lives. And that even if we have family, friends and partners, ultimately we must take responsibility for ourselves and our actions.

Total self-acceptance

And what about the eighth goal on the list – the need for total acceptance?

This is something that many individuals find worrying. They think that if they accept themselves fully, they'll become smug and complacent – and that other people will find them insufferable.

But the reason they worry is that they haven't grasped a vital fact, which is that there's a vast difference between accepting *yourself*, and accepting your *behaviour* and everything that you do.

Self-acceptance is all about recognising that even though you're human, fallible, and bound to make mistakes from time to time, you are still a good person – even if on occasions your *behaviour* is diabolical!

For example, Simon had such a good social life at university that he didn't knuckle down and revise for his first-year exams. Not surprisingly, he failed. Does this make him a bad person? No. Should he hate himself? No. But should he accept that he could have behaved differently? Very definitely yes. And should he take responsibility for sorting out how to re-sit these exams? Oh yes. And should he resolve to learn from this failure? Certainly. Should he apologise to his hard-working parents who have been saving for years in order to help pay for his studies? Absolutely.

So, accepting yourself doesn't mean that you must condone your grumpy behaviour, or your laziness, or your timidity, or your obesity – or anything else that you know you would benefit from altering. All it means is that no matter how much of your behaviour needs changing, you always accept and value yourself.

And when you do that – when you accept the essence of you – you'll find that you're in a position of power, and that you're able to start changing the things about you that you *can* and *want* to change.

In fact, the interesting thing is that the more you accept yourself, the more you'll feel justified in spending time and energy on improving yourself. This will happen because you'll be gaining what I call a 'cushion of confidence'. This is just a feeling: it's a bit like being buoyed up on a cosy cushion of air, which makes you feel more safe and secure in yourself. You'll get your cushion of confidence when you work on accepting and loving yourself – and it will encourage other good feelings, such as a belief that you're just as special as anyone else, a sense that you have the same rights as other people, and that you deserve happiness.

On the other hand, if you're always vilifying yourself whenever you make a mistake, and constantly giving yourself a poor rating, then you're not likely to feel justified in improving yourself. And then things will get worse, and you'll dislike yourself even more. And there will seem even less point in trying to improve yourself and your life. And you will have set up a downward spiral that is enormously difficult to escape from.

Will I become too self-obsessed if I get a good self-esteem habit?

Sometimes, adults with poor self-esteem feel very anxious about the eight goals I've listed. They think that achieving them will mean becoming self-obsessed and that they'll stop caring about other people.

But the truth is that when you have poor self-esteem, you often dwell on the worst in *other* people – not just in yourself. You may be bad-tempered with friends or family who have the same problems as you – just because their difficulties remind you of your own. You may feel enormous resentment towards people who appear to have their lives sorted. And you may even mutter: 'It's all right for her . . .' The assumption being that this other person has it easy and never has to work at anything.

These feelings aren't helpful to other people – and they're not very accepting of them either. Interestingly, as we learn to accept ourselves, to accept that we have rights, and that we're 'allowed' to be happy, healthy and successful, we generally come to the realisation that other people have all these rights too.

If you develop good self-esteem you won't become nastier and more inward looking – quite the reverse. You'll become more calmly confident, more content, and far more accepting of everyone else.

There's a lot of it about!

Poor self-esteem is a hugely widespread problem, particularly in the UK. Why? Well, much of it stems from the way we were brought up.

As children, many of us felt that we had no rights whatsoever. In addition, we were rarely praised in case we got 'big-headed', we were often chastised for being 'bad', and we frequently weren't noticed unless we were doing naughty or annoying things.

Thankfully, nowadays plenty of parents praise their children, and they give them attention even when they're being good. Wisely, they criticise the child's *behaviour* and not the child. They don't say: 'You are a horrible, bad little boy.' Instead, they say: 'I love you very much, but that doesn't mean I'm going to put up with this bad behaviour, so please stop it.'

But this insight is a pretty modern advance – and it still doesn't exist in lots of families. So many readers will recall a childhood where:

- it was considered wrong to be noticeable;
- showing-off was almost a crime;
- it was quite usual to be told you were horrid or nasty or disgusting;
- you were told it was wicked to be angry;
- you could sense that parents and relatives were embarrassed if you were tactile and loving;
- you were encouraged to believe that you shouldn't expect much from life;
- you were criticised or ridiculed if you showed signs of 'getting above yourself' (whatever that was supposed to mean).

Small wonder, then, that there's a lot of poor self-esteem about. It can take a long time to learn to value yourself, when early conditioning constantly relegated the whole *idea* of self to the bottom of the pile.

Worse scenarios

However, there are plenty of other types of upbringing or events in childhood which cause even more damage.

If you were sexually abused as a child, you may well feel that you were robbed of your childhood, and you'll almost certainly have a very poor sense of your own worth as a consequence.

If you had a parent who was depressed, seriously mentally ill, violent, or one who committed suicide – it's unlikely that you'll have grown up with massive self-esteem.

Similarly, you may well undervalue yourself if your parents were alcoholics or on drugs.

All sorts of other factors in your childhood may have resulted in poor self-esteem. For example if:

- you lived in a poorer area than your friends;
- you were taken into care because your birth parents couldn't look after you, or didn't choose to;
- you were overweight – and all your mates were thinner;

- you had some kind of disability which meant you couldn't do games at school, or go out to play with other children.

The list goes on and on. But the confusing thing is that though all these situations can engender poor self-esteem – they don't *always* do so. Many people will be adversely affected. Others won't. It's all a bit bewildering.

Unique response

Take a physical illness like chickenpox. If you're exposed to it, and you haven't had it before, you'll probably get it. You'll know you have it because the rash will be recognisable – certainly to a doctor. It will be diagnosed and it will run its course.

Unfortunately, self-esteem is absolutely nothing like chickenpox! It's not predictable or quantifiable. You can't say definitely what causes it, or who'll get it. You can't even advise people how to avoid it for sure.

We're all different, and so are our responses to our genetic make up and our environment. In a sense, this is what makes us all so fascinating. Every single one of us is unique.

Manifestations

A great number of people suffer from poor self-esteem – but the curious thing is that they don't all manifest this problem in the same way. Far from it.

So, if you see an ageing, timid and lonely woman who hides behind her not very attractive, unstyled hair and who speaks in a whisper, you'll probably decide that she has poor self-esteem. And you'll probably be right – though not necessarily.

Likewise, if you see someone who is attractive and who is the life and soul of the party, you'll almost certainly decide that she has good self-esteem. And yet, she might have a lower estimation of herself than anyone else you know.

Many men and women who are rated as great lovers – because they are unselfish in bed and dedicated to making their partners feel good – are desperately short of self-esteem. They feel they don't deserve to lie back and have good things done to them, and that they don't warrant someone else's time and attention, or love. They try to get a sense of worth by giving great pleasure to someone else. It doesn't work. Not long term. It just leaves them feeling empty inside.

Then there are all the people who avoid promotion, just in case they might have to criticise someone. There are individuals who take menial jobs – even though they're colossally bright – because they're sure they'll fail in a competitive environment, and there are also very able adults who would sooner die than speak up in a meeting – because they're sure that no one wants to hear their opinion. There are also plenty of individuals who blame themselves every time anything goes wrong, because they don't believe that they can ever get things right.

Do any of these descriptions strike a chord with you? If so, you're having a rough time. And you're having it because you don't value yourself, which means that – deep down – you probably feel unlovable, undesirable, stupid, or just different. These are really horrid feelings to have.

Celebrities

Many individuals who have these horrible feelings cover them up by performing in some way. We all know of stars who have triumphed in sport or entertainment, but who clearly don't value *themselves*. They get caught up in a spiral of needing more and more success, and needing to be more and more busy – just because underneath they think they're worthless. They have to keep 'doing' because they're afraid just to 'be'.

Unfortunately the conflict in their minds tends to land them in trouble and they often hit the headlines for the wrong reasons – such as when they're drunk and incapable at awards ceremonies.

Even people born into wealth and nobility can suffer from poor self-esteem. Take the late Princess of Wales: she was charming, beautiful and rich; she could converse with the privileged and the underprivileged alike – and yet she was clearly a person who did not accept or value herself. Her eating disorder is evidence of that. And when it came to her charity work, although she was hugely committed to various causes and gave endless support to them, she somehow gave the impression that she needed these causes as much, if not more, than *they* needed *her*. When they thanked her, or told her how enormously helpful she was to them, she gained a sense of validity and affirmation that was missing from her belief system most of the time. This was her private tragedy, and it was – I'm quite sure – a living nightmare for her.

Where do we go from here?

Step by step, this book will help you to identify your particular areas of low self-esteem. It will also help you to understand why you have them. It will encourage you to make positive changes, so that you can achieve the goals outlined earlier in this chapter.

The changes, as I've already said, will mostly involve learning to alter your feelings about yourself. You will be able to do this by learning how to re-think your thoughts.

Feelings don't come out of the great blue yonder: they are actually *caused* by thoughts. This may come as a surprise to you – but it's true.

For example, you may be at a party and find yourself becoming more and more miserable. You could be forgiven for believing that the party *itself* has made you miserable. But, actually, the reason for your misery is almost certainly a little voice in your head prompting you with unhelpful thoughts such as:

- no one likes me;
- I'm boring;
- I'm hopeless at meeting new people.

. . . And so on. These unhelpful thoughts spring up at the most awkward times. They're recurring thoughts – what I choose to call a Negative Inner Commentary (NIC). And, as you'll see later in the book, it is this commentary that is holding you back and damaging you.

So, to gain a good self-esteem habit, you're going to need to re-think how you think about yourself. To do this, you must learn to identify how you usually think about yourself and to replace those thoughts with more positive ones, or a *Positive* Inner Commentary (PIC).

You'll find this is a real adventure. In fact, there's very little in life that can compare with the exhilaration of re-programming your mind to benefit *you*! Of course, your progress is likely to be a bit up and down, much like being on a roller-coaster. But the end result will be that you'll feel more calmly content and confident than you ever have before.

Brace yourself – you're in for a thrilling ride!

Chapter One Key Points:

1 Good self-esteem comes from liking, valuing, caring for and accepting yourself.
2 To develop a habit of good self-esteem, you need to change how you think, how you feel, how you behave and how you speak about yourself.
3 You can start work today on achieving the eight goals to good self-esteem.
4 It is essential to accept yourself. This does not mean that you have to accept or condone all your behaviour.
5 Fully accepting ourselves leads to us fully accepting other people.
6 Poor self-esteem manifests itself in a wide variety of ways.
7 Our moods and feelings stem from our thoughts.

2

Facing Up to the Problem

This chapter consists of three tests. These tests will show you what the scale of your problem is. They will also show you the areas in your life which are working, and will highlight those which need improvement.

There is no 'right' answer to anything. So please don't just tick the answer you think looks best. There are no prizes here – and you have no need to impress anyone.

I've had clients who've quickly ticked everything that they thought looked good. Perfect relationship, great parenting . . . you name it. In fact, a quick glance at their answers might suggest they had absolutely no need of therapy!

However, after chatting about how they've filled in their answers, it usually becomes apparent that the whole business of 'keeping up appearances' is a major problem. So major, in fact, that they don't dare answer truthfully.

You see, even when some people know that they need help, they often feel compelled to be nice, and not to moan, and to present as intelligent and sprightly an image as possible.

This is all part of a syndrome in insecure people who don't believe they have much value.

With such clients, I spend a lot of time persuading them that during therapy they can feel utterly safe and unjudged. It takes a while for them to accept this, but, in time, they relax, and then they find that they can say things – or admit to feelings – which they've rarely admitted to themselves, let alone to anyone else. Opening up in this way is usually a big relief to people.

You and I are not sitting in a 'safe' consulting room. But I do still urge you to let yourself go and to be as honest as you can with yourself while you work through this book. This will help you in the end. But I would be the first to caution you that it will be hard – at least initially. Some thoughts or characteristics which you uncover might disturb you – or alter your mental image of yourself.

But you've bought this book because you know you want to change some aspects of yourself. Change is difficult – but it's exciting.

Going through life trying to present an invincible image to the world is ultimately much *more* difficult. Pretending that nothing is wrong, even to *yourself*, is utterly exhausting! So this is your chance to listen to the niggles inside you that tell you things are *not* OK – and to pluck up the courage to answer these various tests honestly.

One final thought: Chapter Three will consist of looking back at your results in detail and helping you to see what they mean. Some people find it easier to photocopy the tests – either before or after they do them – so that they don't have to keep turning back to this chapter while they're working on the next one.

Test one

General

1. How much do you like yourself?
(a) A lot (b) Quite a bit (c) Not much (d) Not at all

2. Do you feel you deserve to be happy?
(a) Definitely (b) Partly (c) Not much (d) No

3. Do you feel lovable?
(a) Yes (b) I think so (c) Not very (d) No

4. Do you feel confident about yourself and your future?
(a) Yes (b) Mostly (c) Not very (d) No

5. Do you feel comfortable and confident when with your family?
(a) Very much (b) Usually (c) Rarely (d) Never

6. Do you feel comfortable and confident at work?
(a) Yes (b) Mostly (c) Not really (d) Absolutely not

7. Do you like other people?
(a) Almost always (b) Much of the time (c) Not much (d) Hardly at all

8. In your opinion, do other people tend to like you?
(a) Mostly (b) Sometimes (c) Rarely (d) No

9. Do you feel that you can lead other people, or be in charge?
(a) Mostly (b) Sometimes (c) Rarely (d) Never

10. Do you feel that other people value your opinion?
(a) Yes (b) Usually (c) Not much (d) Never

11. Do you agree with the statement: 'It's only human to make mistakes'?
    (a) Definitely (b) I think so (c) Not really (d) No

12. If *you* make a mistake, can you accept that you're only human and therefore allowed to fail on occasions?
    (a) Definitely (b) Mostly (c) Find this hard (d) No, I can't

13. If you do well at something, do you tend to discount it, rather than congratulate yourself?
    (a) Never (b) Rarely (c) Sometimes (d) Usually

14. If you fail at something, do you 'beat yourself up' over it?
    (a) Rarely (b) Sometimes (c) Usually (d) Always

15. Do you find it difficult to criticise someone to their face if you have to?
    (a) Rarely (b) Sometimes (c) Usually (d) Always

16. Do you find it difficult to accept criticism, even when you know it's justified?
    (a) No (b) Sometimes (c) Usually (d) Always

17. Do you feel inadequate compared with most people?
    (a) No (b) Sometimes (c) Mostly (d) Always

18. If you had to, could you give a speech in public?
    (a) Yes (b) I think so (c) With great difficulty (d) Absolutely not

19. Do you find it hard to say 'no' to people's demands on you?
    (a) No (b) Sometimes (c) Often (d) Always

20. Do you believe that your feelings about yourself hold you back in life?
    (a) I don't feel held back in any way (b) I don't think so (c) Almost certainly (d) Very definitely

Relationships

1. Do you tend to feel that you'll never be in a really good relationship?
   (a) No (b) Sometimes (c) Frequently (d) Always

2. Do you agree with the statement: 'I can only be happy if I'm in a relationship'?
   (a) No (b) A bit (c) A lot (d) Totally

3. Does the idea of ending a relationship fill you with panic and terror?
   (a) No (b) A bit (c) A lot (d) Totally

4. Do you tend to stay in a relationship even if it's an unhappy one?
   (a) No (b) Probably (c) Usually (d) Definitely – anything's better than being alone

5. Do you experience difficulties in finding romance?
   (a) No (b) Not usually (c) Usually (d) I have never had a proper girlfriend/boyfriend/partner

6. Do you agree with the statement: 'I am responsible for my own development, the control of my life, and my ability to be happy whether or not I currently have a partner'?
   (a) Totally (b) I think so (c) Not sure (d) I think this statement is a load of nonsense

7. If you're in a relationship do you find it easy to socialise with your partner's friends?
   (a) Yes (b) Sometimes (c) Not really (d) I find it hard to socialise with *anyone*

8. If your partner enjoys evenings out without you, can you enjoy these evenings too – either quietly alone, or by going out with your own friends?
   (a) Yes (b) Sometimes (c) Not really (d) I feel miserable if he/she socialises without me

9. Do you feel that your partner controls you and the relationship?
   (a) No – it's an equal relationship (b) A bit (c) Mostly (d) Totally

10. Do you find it difficult to put across your point of view when it differs from your partner's?
    (a) No (b) A bit (c) It's really hard (d) I keep quiet – he or she probably knows best

11. Are you the sort of person who tries to keep quiet about differences of opinion but who – from time to time – erupts in furious, or even violent, anger?
    (a) No – I talk about things long before it gets to the stage of being so angry (b) Occasionally (c) Sometimes (d) This often happens and I feel completely out of control when it does

12. If you're in a relationship, do you find it easy to accept love, care and sexual tenderness?
    (a) Definitely (b) Pretty much (c) Not really (d) Not at all

13. Do you like your genitals?
    (a) Yes – they're great (b) They're OK (c) Not really (d) They're ugly

14. Do you offer sex to people so that you'll feel loved – albeit temporarily?
    (a) Absolutely not (b) I don't think so (c) Perhaps sometimes (d) Often

You, your body and your background

1. Do you like your body – its shape, your hair and your facial features?
   (a) Definitely (b) Quite a lot of it (c) Not much of it (d) I hate my body

2. Do you have an eating disorder – i.e., do you try not to eat, do you binge-eat and purge, do you over-eat, or do you think about food almost all of the time?
   (a) No (b) I have a bit of a problem (c) I have a big problem (d) Everything about food is a problem for me

3. If you dislike bits of your body, are you good at making the most of your good features, or at changing those things for the better that *can* be changed?
   (a) Very (b) Quite (c) I try, but it feels like too big a task (d) What's the point?

4. Are you comfortable with the colour of your skin?
   (a) Very (b) Yes (c) Quite (d) No

5. Do you feel that other people respond positively to your appearance?
   (a) Yes (b) Mostly (c) Sometimes (d) No

6. If you have a physical problem or disability is it
   (a) Not too bad (allergy, migraine etc.) (b) Quite serious (chronic back pain, epilepsy, psoriasis . . .) (c) Very serious (you have limbs that don't work, you are blind or deaf, or you have a terminal illness)?

7. If you've answered Question 6, would you say that your disability – however serious it is – makes your life hopelessly difficult?
   (a) Not at all (b) I notice it but am determined to rise above it (c) It's a big problem and I feel lousy because of it (d) It ruins my life

8. Do you have a sense that your cultural or social background is inferior to that of most people?
   (a) Not at all (b) Just a bit (c) Quite a lot (d) Totally

9. Do you honestly feel that other people perceive your cultural or social background as being inferior to theirs?
   (a) No (b) Maybe (c) Almost certainly (d) I am convinced that most people think I come from rubbish

10. Are you proud of what your parents or grandparents achieved – even if by most people's standards they didn't achieve much?
    (a) Very (b) Yes (c) A bit (d) No

Your childhood

1. Was your childhood a happy one?
   (a) Very (b) Mostly (c) Quite (d) Definitely not

2. When you were a child, did your parents/carers give you the impression that you were a lovely, special and delightful child?
   (a) Absolutely (b) Mostly (c) Not really (d) Definitely not

3. Do you feel that your parents had strong feelings of love for you?
   (a) Definitely (b) Mostly (c) Not very (d) Not at all

4. Were you a bully as a child?
   (a) No (b) Don't think so (c) Sometimes (d) Yes

5. Were you bullied as a child by other children?
   (a) No (b) Maybe once (c) Sometimes (d) Constantly

6. Did you feel that your parents/carers supported you when you had problems at school or with other children?
   (a) Definitely (b) Usually (c) Not much (d) Didn't want to know

7. Did you feel unattractive as a child?
   (a) No (b) Occasionally (c) Quite often (d) Usually

8. Do you feel that your parents/carers could have made an effort to help you to look better?
   (a) I felt attractive and they helped me to be that (b) I felt quite attractive – and they always encouraged me to look my best (c) I didn't feel very attractive – but they weren't aware of this (d) I felt unattractive – and they never, ever put themselves out to help me

9. Did a parent die during your childhood?
   (a) No (b) Yes

10. Have either of your parents committed suicide?
   (a) No (b) Yes

11. Did either of your parents abandon you – i.e., did a parent disappear out of your life for a substantial part of your childhood?
   (a) No (b) Yes

12. Did you feel as a child that a birth parent actively disliked you – or couldn't be bothered to be with you, or to care for you?
   (a) No (b) A bit (c) I think so (d) Very definitely

Recent significant events

1. Have you recently ended a relationship?
   (a) No (b) Yes

2. Has someone close to you died in the past two years or so?
   (a) No (b) Yes

3. Have you quarrelled with, or lost touch with, a friend in recent months?
   (a) No (b) Yes

4. Have you lost a job in the last two years or so?
   (a) No (b) Yes

5. Has your partner had an affair with someone else in the past two years or so?
   (a) No (b) Yes

6. Have you (or if you're a guy, has your partner) had a termination in the past two years?
   (a) No (b) Yes

7. Have you had a serious illness or a serious accident in the past two years or so?
   (a) No (b) Yes

8. Has something happened in the past two years or so that has meant you now have much less money than you used to have?
   (a) No (b) Yes

9. Do you tend to go to sleep easily, but wake up early in the morning and find you can't get back to sleep?
   (a) No (b) Yes

Your space, spirituality and lifestyle

1. Do you feel that your life is chaotic?
   (a) No (b) Rarely (c) Often (d) All the time

2. Do you feel very stressed?
   (a) No (b) Sometimes (c) Often (d) Always

3. Do you take some form of exercise for at least twenty minutes three times a week?
   (a) Always (b) Mostly (c) Sometimes (d) No

4. Do you drink more than twenty-one units of alcohol per week if you're a woman or more than twenty-eight units of alcohol if you're a man?
   (a) Never (b) Not often (c) Quite often (d) Always

5. Do you smoke?
   (a) No
   (b) Yes – but less than five cigarettes a week
   (c) Yes – nearly twenty per day
   (d) More than a pack a day

6. Do you have a drug habit that you suspect is getting out of control?
   (a) Don't do drugs at all
   (b) Very occasional user – and then only cannabis
   (c) Am doing more than I was
   (d) Yes – it's definitely getting out of hand

7. Do you believe that you respect yourself – and act as though you do?
   (a) Absolutely
   (b) I think so
   (c) Maybe not enough
   (d) I seem to have lost my self-respect

8. Do you think that other people looking at you would believe you care for and respect yourself?
   (a) Yes
   (b) I hope so
   (c) I doubt it
   (d) No

9. Do you feel you never have time for you?
   (a) No
   (b) Sometimes
   (c) Often
   (d) Yes, definitely

10. Do you have quiet, spiritual times which feed your soul?
   (a) Definitely
   (b) Quite often
   (c) Not much
   (d) There's no time

11. If you feel stressed, do you deliberately find an activity that will de-stress you, such as dance, yoga, meditation etc.?
    (a) Yes (b) Usually (c) Occasionally (d) Never get round to it – not sure these things are quite me

Test two

This test takes the form of a number of scenarios. All you have to do is to choose the answer in each case that best sums up how you would react in such a situation.

(1) A blind man is waiting by the side of a busy road. No one is helping him. You feel very sorry for him. Do you:

    (a) Wander over to him, ask if he wants some help, and if he does, allow him to take your arm and walk him across the road – chatting as you go?
    (b) Feel nervous about asking if he wants help – but go anyway, and ask how you can best help him?
    (c) Carry on walking without helping him. Not because you don't *want* to help, but because you feel you'll do it all wrong, or you fear that helping him will draw attention to yourself – and you can't cope with that?

(2) You're on a bus and a trio of young foreign students get on. They hardly speak any English. They look shy. They don't understand our money – and you see them offer the conductor a ten-pound note for three £1 fares. The conductor tells them he can't change the money and orders them off the bus. It's obvious they are upset – and also that they don't understand what is going on. Do you:

(a) Intervene immediately. Go up to the conductor, tell him that you will not allow him to eject these kids from the bus, that you're appalled by his behaviour, and insist that he gives them change?
(b) Fume about what is happening but don't feel you can take the conductor on in person. However, you take his number, make a note about the time and place of the incident and report him to his company when you get home. But nevertheless feel that you should have helped the kids more and you wish you'd acted more decisively?
(c) Wish you could do (a) or even (b) but you can't find the courage. Instead you berate yourself for your cowardice and worry about the incident all night?

(3) You are late for a doctor's appointment. The truth is that you left late and that you did not leave enough time for the journey. There were road works on the way, but you still acknowledge that if you had organised yourself better you would have been in time. When you get to the surgery, your slot has gone. Do you:

(a) Apologise and say that you realise you simply did not leave enough time for unpredictable factors like road works. Then say that you appreciate the doctor is busy, but wonder if the receptionist can fit you in later if you wait around?
(b) Say: 'It wasn't my fault. I left in plenty of time and there were road works. It's not fair, the doctor *must* see me.' Then get angry so that the receptionist is angry with *you*, makes no effort to fit you in that day, and says you'll have to make a completely fresh appointment?
(c) Feel so bad about getting so behind that you don't even go in for the appointment, but go home feeling hopeless and upset with yourself and the world?

(4) A teacher corners you as you pick up your little boy from school. She asks if you'll run a stall at the fête on Saturday afternoon. You have a busy Saturday planned. Your parents are expecting

to see you, your husband has asked for some time to himself to play football for the local team (which means you'll have to look after all three of your kids); and your daughter has a swimming lesson which will involve you driving her to the pool. Do you:

(a) Say, firmly: 'Sorry, I'm afraid you'll have to count me out. There are far too many things happening that day to cram in any more, but I'll buy some scones for the cake stall and get them to you during Saturday morning'?
(b) Offer lots of excuses as to why you can't do it. Realise you've sounded rattled and feel worried that the teacher doesn't believe you, will not like you – and that she may take it out on your son, so the next day you take in a case of wine, that you can ill afford, for the bottle stall?
(c) Hear yourself say 'yes', knowing that you shouldn't have agreed and so are now deeply worried about what excuses you're going to offer your parents and your husband, who are all going to feel that you've let *them* down?

(5) You go to see a doctor. He is not someone you've consulted before. Your problem is not serious, but you find it worrying. This doctor is extremely kind to you – takes all the time in the world – and gives you the impression that you're someone worth bothering about. Do you:

(a) Feel very heartened by the consultation, feel pleased that a professional person has given you so much time and attention, that it was certainly worth going, and you feel better?
(b) Feel quite tearful. The unexpected kindness has triggered something in you. You feel unsettled by it. You're not sure how to handle it. The encounter makes you feel that something in your own personal life must be missing for you to be so touched by the kindness of a stranger who is paid to see you?

(c) Feel deeply unsettled. This kindness is something you long for – but don't know how to find. Perhaps you start day-dreaming about the doctor. You even start wondering if the doctor could be keen on you. Intellectually, you know this cannot be true but the consultation has stirred up feelings about being wanted and cared for that are both appealing and frightening?

Test three

How you rate yourself

In this test, I am simply going to ask you to give yourself a number of ratings. In Chapter Three I'll be explaining why these tests are useful and how you can check that the rating you're giving yourself is accurate.

In each test, there's a long horizontal line with 0 per cent at one end and 100 per cent at the other. What you have to do is to decide where your rating is on that line.

Let me give you an example of how to tackle this: my nephew loves cartoons and comics, and so I asked him to rate a couple of his favourite characters. I told him that 0 per cent meant that he didn't like them at all; 100 per cent meant that he thought they were fantastic. I then asked him how much he likes the character of Superman.

'A lot,' he said.

'Is he your favourite?' I asked.

'No.' He laughed. 'My very best favourite is Dennis the Menace. But Superman's still cool.'

So I asked him how many marks out of a hundred he would give to Dennis.

'A hundred!' he said.

'And how many would Superman get?'

'About ninety.'

So then I got him to draw a cross on the line below – where Superman and Dennis the Menace should go.

0% **100%**

x x

S D

Superman was towards the right-hand end of the line; Dennis the Menace was as far to the right as you can go. We could have gone on, making crosses to represent the ratings of other cartoon characters.

Now, I'd like you to put crosses on the lines below to show how you rate yourself in a number of different ways:

(a) Rate how worthwhile you are

In this section, I'd like you to give yourself a rating for how worthwhile a person you think you are. Before you make a cross on the line below, take note that 0 per cent would be the rating for someone whose behaviour was so terrible that you felt he or she was not at all worthwhile. And 100 per cent would be reserved for someone with exemplary behaviour who contributes so hugely to life that they're seen as an absolute saint. Where will you put yourself? When you've had a think, make your cross.

0% **100%**

(b) Rate how lovable you are

For the second rating, decide who you think is the most lovable person you know – or have heard about – and then come up with someone who you think has virtually no lovable qualities at all. These people would get 100 per cent and 0 per cent respectively. How lovable are you in comparison? Have a think, and then rate yourself on the line below.

0% **100%**

(c) Rate how capable you are

Tackle this in exactly the same way. And make your cross.

0% **100%**

(d) Rate how good a friend you are

Lastly, on the line below, give yourself a rating for how good a friend you are.

0% **100%**

Now move on to Chapter Three to see what all these tests mean for you.

3

Your Own Personal Assessment

Now, if you can have your test results from Chapter Two to hand, we can see just how you did.

Test one

This is a very long test with seventy-six questions in it, divided up into six sections, so I'm not going to exhaust you by giving an analysis of every single answer.

As you can imagine, all these questions yield very individual results, so it's not possible to address every single reader's answers in detail. However, the real purpose of Test One is to open your eyes to specific difficulties you haven't previously identified – and also to help you discover where your main problems lie.

Hopefully, you may already have a clearer idea of which parts of your life need the most improvement. This is the first step in a process which will see you becoming the world-expert on *you*, and this is what your aim should be. Once you know yourself better, you can start making changes where you want to. And you can start making them *now*!

Generally speaking – and you've probably worked this out for yourself – in Test One, when you select (a) as your answer, you demonstrate that you have a very positive attitude and generous quantities of self-value.

If you pick (b) it means you don't regard yourself with wholehearted approval, but you still have quite a healthy view of yourself. Answers that get a (c) show that you're not very happy, and that you have considerable problems with your sense of self-worth. And if you plump for (d), this indicates that your self-esteem is poor.

Let's now progress through each section of Test One in turn. All your answers should tell you something useful, but I'm going to draw your attention to those that will probably have most significance for you.

General

Question 1: How much do you like yourself?

Even the most supremely confident person bursting with self-regard might hesitate to answer (a) – 'A lot' – in response to the question. I suspect most individuals with good self-esteem will modestly tick the (b) answer – 'Quite a bit'. This is OK – especially if you're British and not much given to self-congratulation!

But if your answer is (c), 'Not much', this is *not* OK. In fact, there's definitely room for improvement.

If you've answered (d), 'Not at all' – please stop and think whether you *really* mean this or not. Are you saying that there's nothing whatsoever about you that you like? *Nothing at all*? If this is the case, it is important that you make an appointment with your doctor, because you may very likely be suffering from depression, and will need more help than that given in this book.

By all means take your scores along when you see him or her. Your doctor will discuss the possibilities of medication and/or counselling with you.

Question 5: Do you feel comfortable and confident when with your family?

It's quite common for someone with more positive answers elsewhere to have a (c) rating – or even a (d) here. Families are a rich source of trouble where self-esteem is concerned – and if you have problems with your family, you should find Chapter Four particularly helpful when you get to it.

Question 6: Do you feel comfortable and confident at work?

If you have chosen to answer with a (c) or a (d), then you hardly need me to tell you that this is a distinctly difficult area of your life which needs urgent attention. This is especially true if your answers elsewhere in this section are more healthy. Many individuals who apparently have quite good self-esteem, and who cope well with relationships and social occasions, feel very nervous and uncertain at work. This is usually because they have little regard for their own abilities. Does this sound like you? If so, perhaps you should ask yourself whether your unease would apply to all work situations, or whether you are simply unhappy in your current job, but have so far felt unable to leave it.

Question 8: In your opinion, do other people tend to like you?

If you don't feel that people like you, and you have circled (c) or (d), I want to encourage you to challenge your answer right now. Are you really sure that your assessment of people's reactions to you is correct?

Liking people and being liked are common problem areas in individuals with poor self-esteem, which is why we'll be returning to them time and time again. For now, just try and open your mind to the possibility that your perception of people's regard for you may be a bit skewed.

Question 12: If you make a mistake, can you accept that you're only human, and therefore allowed to fail on occasions?

When people answer this question with a (c) or (d), it's a clear indicator that they are far too harsh on themselves. It also shows up a tendency for unrealistic perfectionism, which can never be lived up to. So if this applies to you, take it from me that your self-esteem is never going to be great while you demand higher standards from yourself than you do from other people – because you're inevitably going to feel disappointed.

People with poor self-esteem frequently forgive others for mistakes while withholding forgiveness for themselves. This is damaging. Try to accept that while you may dislike making mistakes, it's not the end of the world if you do!

Question 13: If you do well at something, do you tend to discount it, rather than congratulate yourself?

This question, much like Question 12, highlights the kind of double standard operated by many people with poor self-regard. Such individuals will admire someone else's achievements, but dismiss their own. Do you do this? If so, it's time to try treating yourself with the same admiration and generosity that you extend to others.

The remaining questions in this first section are all about assertiveness and speaking up for yourself. If you can see that you have particular problems in this area, you'll find there's plenty of advice to help you in Chapter Nine.

Relationships

Let us now look at your answers in the Relationships section.

The vast majority of people who come to me for therapy come because they're upset about a relationship.

Many of them actually have all sorts of problems quite separate from their love lives. But it's the relationship – or lack of one – that drives them to seek help; not their self-esteem, or their depression, or their stress.

So it's a reasonable assumption that many people who decide to buy a self-help book like *Get the Self-Esteem Habit* are also worried about a relationship. And you may be such a person.

Now because relationships are at the hub of how we feel about ourselves, it's quite possible that this section will highlight distress over what is happening in your private life. Indeed, you may score far more dismally in this part of the quiz than anywhere else. If this is so, don't worry. It just means you've got some very specific work to do. But I think you know that.

Question 2: Do you agree with the statement: 'I can only be happy if I'm in a relationship'?

If you've answered anything other than (a), it means that you have little confidence in yourself as a single person. If you have no conviction that your life is important and viable irrespective of whether or not you have a partner, then you're never going to value yourself properly.

Much the same applies to Questions 3 and 4. If you've answered (c) or (d) to either or both of them, it means that you're too hung up on the status of being in a relationship and that you therefore tend to remain in one even if it's miserable.

The reason for this kind of belief and behaviour is likely to be tied up with your Negative Inner Commentary, which you can learn about in Chapter Five.

Question 5: Do you experience difficulties in finding romance?

Shy people will score badly here. But something can always be done about shyness. For a start, you can learn some techniques which will help you to look and feel *less* shy, and you'll find those in Chapter Eight. But, on a deeper level, your shyness will lessen the more you learn to regard yourself with love and acceptance – and this will happen as you work on the book as a whole.

Question 6: Do you agree with the statement: 'I am responsible for my own development, the control of my life and my ability to be happy whether or not I currently have a partner'?

This is the most important question in the section. If you can agree with the statement that you are responsible for your own life and happiness, this indicates emotional maturity. When you believe this, life becomes easier and relationships are formed for the right reasons and not out of desperation. So: (a) is the only really good answer to Question 6, (b) is fair, (c) is not good and (d) means that you really have a need to overhaul your basic mindset. This is obviously a tough challenge. But it's not impossible. People do it. And you can be one of them.

There will, by the way, be some readers who have answered (c) or (d) to Question 6 but who are actually in a good relationship. Such people may wish to disagree with my view that feeling responsible for yourself is desirable. They may protest that a happy relationship gives you everything that you need, and that it's healthy to lean on another person.

Do you feel this? If you do, I would ask you this: *How anxious do you feel that your relationship may go wrong? And that if it does, you'll be very cast down – perhaps even destroyed?*

I am prepared to bet that deep down you often feel anxiety about this and that you frequently worry about:

- how much your partner loves you;
- whether he or she is bored with you;
- whether he or she will stay with you;
- whether he or she is faithful to you.

If this is the case, perhaps you will concede that you would feel more calmly confident in your relationship if you did not require your partner to 'make you happy' – but instead looked to yourself for that.

Of course your partner can enhance your happiness – quite wonderfully, I hope. But he or she should not be responsible for it. Have a think about this.

Question 11: Are you the sort of person who tries to keep quiet about differences of opinion, but who – from time to time – erupts in furious, or even violent anger?

This is all about being assertive, as opposed to becoming aggressively angry. Being assertive means that you can stand up for yourself – and your rights – without getting angry. Any score other than an (a) here indicates that you've got a problem.

It's common for individuals who don't have much self-regard to have difficulties in being assertive. Many such people fail to speak up when they're first irritated. Instead, they simmer with annoyance, then they heat up to a state of fury, and eventually – in a rage – they boil over, like an out-of-control pressure cooker. This kind of eruption rarely achieves anything positive: instead it tends to make the angry person look and feel out of control and can result in serious trouble.

Ten years ago, I was the agony aunt on a tabloid newspaper which was mostly read by men. Some of the guys who wrote to me were in prison – having been jailed for violent crimes. A common theme among them was that they had no calm and normal way of expressing their needs and feelings.

Gary – not his real name – wrote: 'My wife was much better with words than me. When we had rows she always won because I couldn't think of the right words to say, or if I did, I was slow in saying them. Trouble was, I got angry when I couldn't make my point, and then I would knock her about. That's what landed me in here. I really regret how I was. She's divorced me – and now I have no wife, no kids and everything's about as bloody as it can get.'

Making your voice count – in a calm but firm way – is vital in building your self-esteem. It will stop you getting unreasonably and destructively angry, because you'll learn how to make your point long before things get out of hand.

Question 12: If you're in a relationship, do you find it easy to accept love, care and sexual tenderness?

Many people who, on the surface, seem confident and capable have enormous problems in being on the receiving end of love and sexual caresses. If you've scored a (c) or a (d) here, you do have a problem with feeling deserving of intimacy, but you can start helping yourself immediately.

Try asking yourself why you *don't* deserve love and good sex. Can you think of a very good reason? You probably can't – but you may remain convinced that you are undeserving.

Try asking yourself:

- Does your partner (if you have one) deserve love and good sex?
- Does your best friend?
- Does your favourite work colleague deserve these things?

The chances are that you'll admit that these people do deserve love and good sex. So why don't you? Are you really so much more horrid, stupid or unlovable than anyone else? I don't think so!

We'll be coming back to this subject, but meanwhile let these thoughts take root in your brain, and you'll get some improvement underway.

Another thing you can do is to make a huge effort to bite back words of self-criticism.

When Maisie gets a new man, she says things like: 'You don't have to take me out for dinner – I'm nobody.' Or: 'I can't believe you want to go to bed with me, my tummy's so fat.'

Does any of this sound like you, I wonder? If it does, please take it from me that you're giving out signals that you see yourself as worthless. And when you do that, you encourage other people to think you're worthless too.

Question 13: Do you like your genitals?

Men tend to have a much more positive view of their genitals than women. Of course some guys would like to add an inch here or there to their manhood, but, on the whole, their genitals are their favourite bits.

Women are different. And vast numbers of the fair sex actively dislike this part of their bodies.

If you're a woman and you've always thought your genitals were ugly, I do urge you to think again. Take a mirror. Have a look. Remind yourself how this part of your body can give infinite pleasure to you and others and how it can also deliver human life. Isn't it all rather miraculous? This is a very important part of you. And as you strive to love yourself in more general terms, it will help if you also learn to see the beauty and charm in your most secret places.

Question 14: Do you offer sex to people so that you'll feel loved – albeit temporarily?

This final question in the Relationships section is all about trying to buy affection. If you've answered with a (c) or (d), then please try to stop the rot right now. Partners will not value you if you try to 'buy' short-term closeness in this way. Sex is special. Keep it for people you care about and who really care for you. If you don't, you'll find it much harder to develop an appropriate sense of love and regard for yourself.

You, your body and your background

I'm going to deal with this third section of Test One in quite general terms.

Obviously, as in all the other sections, (a) is the healthiest answer to give. But if you've answered (b) to most questions, then you haven't too much to worry about.

However, if you have ringed mostly (c)s in this section, then your body – and maybe also your culture or your background – is playing a large part in undermining your own self-value.

If you have scored (d)s, then you have major problems in this area.

It may well be that you have an eating disorder, in which case, please get some additional support or treatment, as I am not covering your difficulty in sufficient depth to get you well. You'll find some pointers for more help in the Help Yourself Guide at the end of this book.

Factors to do with our bodies can usually be divided into things we can alter – and things that we can't.

We all have features that it's impossible to change, but we have far more that we *can* change.

If you can identify – and act upon – what you *can* alter, there's a good chance that your view of yourself and your body will improve. In fact, there's hardly anybody – no matter what problems they perceive they have with their appearance – who can't make some adjustments for the better.

Obviously, there are no magic wands available here. And I don't want to glibly gloss over the fact that a minority of the readers of this book may well have profound disabilities or illnesses that I can't possibly advise them about. But I'm not being patronising when I say that, even in dire circumstances, it is usually possible to make some changes that will help a person feel or look better.

As I write this book, my mother is rapidly going downhill with Alzheimer's disease. She doesn't know me. Neither does she know how old she is, or what anyone said to her two seconds ago. Sadly, she has also lost control of – and interest in – most basic functions.

Now, we could all neglect such demented people – reasoning that they don't know or care what's happening to them. But we don't. We are aware of what used to matter to them, even if they no longer have any sense of it themselves. So we try to make sure that the person is fed and warmly clothed, that someone washes her (or him) and her hair – and maybe even puts some make-up on her, or paints her nails from time to time.

This is all about that person's dignity and rights. We also hope that somehow – in what's left of the working brain – the dementia sufferer will feel better for *looking* better. We also know that other people respond more positively to individuals who are pleasing to the eye, and who don't smell of dirt, or urine.

As a reader of this book, you are most unlikely to be suffering from dementia. But you may well be someone who feels very unattractive, and you may feel that you don't have the energy to make any improvements. This is probably because you look at the whole picture and feel that it is too much to cope with.

But why not start making a difference, right now, in a small way?

Make a list of what you *could* change about your appearance – and then resolve to make just one small change *this week*. Starting is always the most difficult bit. Once you've begun one task to improve how you look, you will find it easier to tackle the next thing on your list. Try it.

This section about our bodies and our backgrounds also encompasses our ethnic culture and background.

Most of us have some pride in our heritage. And yet we're also likely to have reservations about it too. Maybe we don't feel our ancestors were very honourable on occasions. Sometimes it's hard to face up to those things.

We might also find it hard to deal with the wrongs that were done to people of our culture at various times in history.

No matter what our background, good self-esteem depends on acceptance of our heritage as part of ourselves. In other words, we need to find things in our cultural past that we can identify with, and feel proud of.

Many people with problems of poor self-esteem dislike what they come from. This might be to do with race, or class – but is more commonly about family characteristics. Is this one of your problems?

You might dislike the fact that your father was a bully – and worry that you've inherited his aggressive genes. Perhaps you wish that your grandparents had made more of their lives and been more ambitious – reasoning that had they been so, life would have been a whole lot easier for you.

Other readers will have much worse things in their backgrounds to contend with. I remember meeting two young adults whose parents had been convicted of mass murder. Their lives were tinged with unimaginable horror, and yet they were re-building them with great bravery.

You may, perhaps, have a huge problem with family members

who sexually abused you – and you may really hate the fact that you are related to such people.

Nothing can take away the fact that you were abused – and there is never, ever, any excuse for it. The adult is always the person at fault. Furthermore, there is no reason at all why you should ever forgive the crime that was inflicted upon you. But it may help you to accept that even an abuser is likely to have some personal qualities that are good – and to look for those qualities in your own nature.

Human beings have the capacity for great resilience. So, if you come from a background that you despise, first of all make quite sure that it really was as bad as you think. Often – even in the worst scenarios – there was some goodness; something worthy of note or praise. Then remember that you – you with your own mind, your own fingerprints and your own DNA – are entirely unique. This is important and it will help you accept that although you – as we all do – have components from your family within you, you can be different.

Most vitally of all, try to accept that you have as much of a right as anyone else to be on this planet – and to be happy.

Your childhood

Most experts would agree that the seeds of poor self-esteem are sown in childhood. So I would expect that a sizeable proportion of readers will have answered (c) or even (d) to many questions in this section. But let's look at the most important answers.

Question 2: When you were a child, did your parents/carers give you the impression that you were a lovely, special and delightful child?

Anything other than (a) – Absolutely – means that you did not feel sufficiently affirmed as a child. And when you don't feel affirmed, you start life with a big disadvantage.

Question 3: Do you feel, looking back, that your parents had strong feelings of love for you?

Again, the only positive answer is (a). Anything less than that leaves a big question mark over how much you were authentically loved. All our early learning about love stems from how our parents loved us. If we did not perceive ourselves as lovable when we were children, this can leave us feeling very vulnerable in later life.

Chapter Four will open your eyes to the sort of parenting you had – and will help you come to terms with it. Chapter Five will help you to see that these early feelings and beliefs can be challenged, and that you can triumph over them.

Question 4: Were you a bully as a child?

It may surprise you to know that bullies frequently have even lower self-esteem than those whom they bully. If you were a bully, I'm sure you're not proud of it. But remember that you probably learned this kind of behaviour from aggressive and insecure family members. It's unlikely that you were a happy child, and so it's important that you forgive yourself now.

Question 5: Were you bullied as a child by other children?

Plenty of people have been bullied at some point – even if only for a short time. But those with little self-regard will tend to have had a more constant problem. Unfortunately, in childhood, it's easy to become a victim. And if you found it difficult to be assertive as a child, I'm sure you had a very tough time.

Question 6: Did you feel that your parents/carers supported you when you had problems at school or with other children?

Your childhood is unlikely to have been easy if you had parents who were lacking in assertive skills, or who thought that a bit of bullying wouldn't do you any harm. I'm afraid that some parents have a lot to answer for. So if you got little or no help from home then you'll almost certainly have answered (c) or (d) to this question.

Unfortunately, you can't alter the past, but you *can* alter how you think about it. Even though you may have been bullied, and even though you may have received no help and support at the time, it's not too late to stop the rot.

Are you still someone who feels pushed around and do you feel that you can never stand up for yourself or calmly make your point? If so, you can improve the situation by changing how you think about yourself (Chapter Five) and learning some assertiveness skills (Chapter Nine).

Question 8: Do you feel that your parents could have made an effort to help you to look better?

The answer to this question may indicate that not only did you feel unattractive as a youngster, but also that you blame your parents for not helping you to look better.

I hope that Chapter Four will give you some help with these feelings. But, as an adult, it's important that you now take responsibility for your own appearance. Remember, it's generally easier to make improvements to how you *look*, than it is to improve how you *think* and *feel*. Don't let anger about your parents' ineptitude in this department hold you back in your life now.

Question 9: Did a parent die during your childhood?

Most of us have not suffered the horror or distress of losing either a mother or a father as a child, but those who have will have found that their life was never the same again after that sad event.

Judging from the clients I've seen who were bereaved as kids, the premature death of a parent seems to leave people feeling more vulnerable than their peers. Not surprisingly, they are more aware than the rest of us that seriously bad things *can* happen in life. One client described her father's death as 'losing a layer of emotional skin that never grows back' – which I think puts it very well.

However, it would be quite wrong to suggest that everyone who – while still a child – experiences the loss of a parent, ends up with poor self-esteem. This is not the case. In fact, if the parent who died was a positive, loving and affirming parent, then the bereaved child can still grow up with bags of positive self-regard. It's true that he or she may feel a life-long residue of sadness which may well surface when a relationship ends – or even during happy times like getting married or having a baby – but most individuals cope with that. And the experience of parental loving – even if it is cut short – is still a great basis for a mentally healthy life.

Question 10: Have either of your parents committed suicide?

Suicide is a completely different issue. Most people who've experienced it within the family are left with a plethora of uncomfortable feelings, including guilt and anger. Although they may, as adults, reason that the parent who took his or her own life was disturbed or ill, this doesn't seem to help the gut feeling that the parent was selfish and simply didn't *care* enough about the family to go on living.

If you had a mother or father who committed suicide, you may well have had great support and love from the other parent and other family members. But if you know that the suicide is still a big issue with you, I do strongly urge you to get some help with it now. A good starting point would be your GP, or a support group for the bereaved. See Chapter Thirteen for more details.

Question11: Did either of your parents abandon you – i.e. did a parent disappear out of your life for a substantial part of your childhood?

Nowadays, a large number of readers will answer 'Yes' to this question. This is because divorce is much more common than in previous generations; and in the aftermath of a marital split, one parent – usually a dad – may disappear for a period.

It's important to realise that this 'disappearance' does not necessarily mean he didn't love you or want to see you. He may have been stopped from doing so.

Frequently, the parent who actually lives with the children is very hurt after the breakdown of a relationship and, in their distress, will make the children's contact with the other parent very difficult. This is usually a conscious decision, though sometimes I think people don't realise they're doing it.

Through the years, I've heard countless tales – usually from men – about how they drove a hundred miles or more to see their kids, only to be met by their ex at the gate saying that the children were with friends, or ill, or just didn't want to come out.

I've also heard heartbreaking stories about Christmas or birthday cards and presents being returned unopened. This is devastating for a parent who already feels side-lined in his children's lives. He is likely to feel angry and frustrated too at his growing suspicion that his offspring are being told he's forgotten them, when he's actually doing his utmost to maintain contact.

Unfortunately, it's very difficult for the visiting parent to fight this kind of determined campaign.

Many fathers – the official estimate is something around 50 per cent – lose contact with their children within two years of divorce or separation.

Now I'm not saying that all of these parents are saints and that the broken marriage or relationship is nothing to do with them. Nor am I denying that some parents do actually walk away from their kids permanently without a backward glance. But they are in the minority.

You may be the adult 'child' of a relationship which broke down. One of your parents may have disappeared out of your life, and you may have been told – by the parent you lived with – that your other parent couldn't be bothered with you. As an adult, it's important to check your facts. You may be carrying a burden of feeling unwanted that is a *false* burden. Maybe this other parent was forced out of the picture, but still loves you very much indeed.

Question 12: Did you feel as a child that a birth parent actively disliked you – or couldn't be bothered to be with you, or to care for you?

Anything other than a firm 'No' shows that you have quite a big issue with your parenting.

If you lived with a parent who had no time for you, or even

appeared to actively dislike you, then I'm sure you suffered greatly as a child – and you probably feel you're still suffering. Perhaps you had brother or sisters who were treated in the same way as you were – and perhaps you youngsters became closer as a result. If that was the case, you may have helped each other to develop some self-worth even though your parents – for whatever reason – weren't doing their job in affirming and loving you properly.

If, on the other hand, you were an only child, or if you were singled out for more criticism or unkindness or neglect than the others, then only *you* can know the full horror of that.

Some parents can't cope with children who are different from them. For example, a sports-mad dad may appear to dislike his artistic, sweet-natured son.

In some families, the difficulties are exacerbated because the male parent actually wonders if the child he doesn't like much is not *his*. This happens far more frequently than people realise – and, of course, sometimes the suspicions are well-founded.

Obviously, if you suspect that this might be the case, this is a big can of worms to open. However, some people do opt to open it and find out more, because they decide that discovering a concrete reason for a parent's attitude makes the attitude easier to live with. Is it possible that your biological dad is someone other than the 'dad' who brought you up? Do you want to know? Will your mother tell? These are very difficult areas, but for a minority of readers they could be of crucial importance.

Sometimes there are other reasons for parental coldness towards a child. A woman who suffers terrible pain when giving birth may never bond with that infant. A man who felt forced into marriage because of an unwanted pregnancy might resent the baby who 'trapped' him. And when relationships deteriorate after the birth of children, as they quite often do, the kids can be 'blamed' for that too – albeit unconsciously.

If you want to find out if there's a reason in your past for one, or both, of your parents' attitudes to you, it's going to take some detective work, and it could also cause family rows and rifts. But if you believe that you'd feel better about your childhood, and about yourself, by uncovering a reason for the way you were treated, then you may want to try to ferret out the truth.

In all these situations, I would advise caution. I would also ask you to ensure that you've got someone in your life – whether it's a partner, another relative, a friend, a minister of religion, or a counsellor – who can live this with you and be there whenever you want to talk about what you're going through. These are hot issues, so don't handle them without the emotional insulation of at least one other person who is on your side 100 per cent.

It may be that you were abandoned by your parents altogether, and perhaps ended up in care or were put up for adoption. Many such children actually have at least one viable birth parent who *could* have looked after them, but for some reason chose not to. The legacy of knowing that a natural parent didn't want you is a monumental grief to bear. It's something that never quite goes away, and I think it's one of the worst tragedies to try to get over. It's bad enough if a parent dies, or is prevented from seeing you; it's quite another if a parent *chooses* not to bring you up.

This is so serious that I feel counselling is called for. It's hard to accept that you were abandoned – even if you were subsequently adopted very happily. You're almost bound to feel huge anger and loss. But you can be helped with this, and you can gradually find a network of support elsewhere.

Whether you grew up with a parent who disliked you or you were actually abandoned, you can come to an understanding that some people – namely your birth mum and/or dad – were lousy at being parents.

This is deeply regrettable. But it is probable that they were immature, hurt, or damaged people themselves with considerable problems. In other words, they were not totally bad individuals, even though their behaviour to you was utterly appalling.

More importantly, their rejection of you *doesn't* mean that you are horrible, unlovable or undesirable. And it definitely doesn't mean that you should reject yourself.

Recent significant events

All the questions in this section are about change – and loss.

At such times, we can feel pretty shaky and vulnerable. We can even feel worthless – especially if these recent events have had strong echoes with previous losses that we've never quite got over.

So, for example, if your long-term partner has just walked out on you, you may feel unworthy, unattractive and uncared for. On top of which you may, in your hurt, have decided that no one else will ever want you again. And yet you can't possibly know this – unless you've got a crystal ball that I don't know about!

The truth is that when you get over the incredible sadness that you're feeling, you'll probably realise that you're OK, and that life can be just as good as it was before – perhaps even better. It will be different, of course, but 'different' doesn't have to mean 'worse'.

In fact, as they get over this kind of trauma, many people find hidden depths within themselves, and they realise that they actually like and approve of themselves more than they realised. Indeed, they'll frequently discover that the relationship itself was denting their self-esteem, and that after grieving for the loss of it, they actually feel better than they have for years. Of course, this doesn't happen overnight.

Whatever your loss, please reach out to friends, an appropriate support group (see the last chapter in this book), or to your doctor.

Now, let's look at a couple of questions in this section that may have special significance.

Question 6: Have you (or if you're a guy, has your partner) had a termination in the past two years?

This question about recent termination is particularly important as it's a subject that crops up time and again with people who are experiencing emotional difficulties in life.

Often the termination seems to unsettle someone greatly – and it stirs up a lot of other issues.

For women in the under-thirty-five age group, this trauma is often hard to understand.

They've been brought up with the idea that a termination is a woman's right which was fought for – and won – by women in the 1960s and 1970s. And that it's quite an easy thing to go through. But they tell me time and time again that they were completely unprepared for the emotional aftermath.

If you have a termination in your recent background, do consider getting some help with your feelings. You'll find useful details in the last chapter.

Question 9: Do you tend to go to sleep easily but wake early in the morning and find you can't go back to sleep?

This question about your sleep patterns is quite significant. If this is happening to you, you should definitely see your GP. Early morning waking is a classic symptom of depression, so please don't try and struggle on alone. Do go and talk to your doctor – or to a qualified counsellor.

Your space, spirituality and lifestyle

The questions in this section – and your answers – should show you at a glance where you are causing yourself stress, and where your life is unbalanced.

Now, you may think that what you drink, or how much you work or exercise, has little to do with self-esteem. But it does, because if you have little self-regard then you're unlikely to look after yourself properly. And if you don't look after yourself, you'll give out a message to everyone around you that you don't care for, or respect, yourself much. And when you do that, you encourage people to think it's OK to *treat* you badly – and this, in turn, will make you feel even less good about yourself.

So, make no mistake about it, people who estimate themselves highly, look after themselves.

Now, we all have hectic periods. We all have times when we can't exercise, or when we have to work late on some project or another, or when we have a tendency to smoke or drink too much. But these bad habits can *become* a habit. And when they do, they damage you.

So, look carefully at this section and decide how balanced your lifestyle is – and how it looks to other people.

If you need to make improvements, and you do unless you've circled the answer (a) in every case, then make a list of how you can. Don't, however, make the mistake of trying to improve everything at once. It'll be far too daunting and you'll only get discouraged. Just change one aspect of your unbalanced lifestyle at a time. Then give yourself credit for it – and when that's sorted, make another improvement.

Step by step, you'll create better habits, and this will increase your sense of self-esteem.

Questions 9 and 10 are all about having time for yourself and about your spirituality. We all need time to feed our inner beings – whether it's through conventional religion, meditation, simple quietness, being by the sea, listening to great music, wandering round art galleries or whatever. It's not for me to dictate how you should do it, but I hope you'll find a way. Achieving a state of calm, loving acceptance of yourself is impossible if you neglect this vital component.

In *Get the Happiness Habit* I wrote about a little technique called the Speedy (ten-minute) Soother, in which you spend ten minutes every day lying or sitting alone – and doing nothing but breathing.

Since the publication of this book, plenty of stressed individuals have told me that though this seems like a good idea, they can't find the time to do it. Just in case you're thinking along the same lines, here's my answer to you:

If you can't set aside ten minutes a day for yourself, then you're not trying. EVERYONE can find ten minutes. If you're saying that you can't find the time, what you really mean is that you WON'T find the time, which is not the same thing at all.

This is a crucial point. Some people – particularly those with poor self-esteem – need to feel that they're busier than everyone else. They believe – albeit unconsciously – that they get increased status or approval from this impression of seething activity.

This is a fallacy. Individuals who can't find ten minutes for themselves give out an air of desperation and stress. Far from being perceived as productive, or capable, or important, they're generally seen as ridiculously disorganised and rather sad.

So, if your initial response to the idea of the Speedy Soother is one of panic – or if you're convinced that this stress-busting technique might be OK for other folk but you're too busy to even contemplate it – then I ask you to examine your motives.

We'll return to this subject in Chapter Ten.

In conclusion, let me reiterate that your answers are a clear indicator of where your various problems lie. You might want to go back and look at your results and my comments before moving on to the results of Tests Two and Three.

Test two

These scenarios are about how you interact with other people in particular situations. Your answers will indicate to you where your difficulties lie. Then all you have to do is learn how to deal with them!

Scenario 1: The one about taking the blind man across the road

Most readers would like to answer (a), but the vast majority of people I've tested answer (b) or even (c).

If this includes you, this doesn't mean you're a bad, horrible, lousy person. But it does mean you're shy and lacking in confidence.

And yet, if you do approach the blind man, what's the worst that can happen?

Maybe you fear that he will turn down your offer of help. Well, that's not so terrible. No one who notices is going to blame you. If they think about it at all – and most people are far too busy with where they're going themselves to be very bothered – they're simply going to think that the blind guy is very determined and ruggedly independent, and that you're a very decent person who was simply trying to help.

Is there any other anxiety you have about helping this man?

Plenty of individuals worry that they might 'do it wrong'. In other words, they won't know how to help. Well, why *should* you know? Being willing to help, but not knowing how, just proves you're kind, but human. So ask the blind man *if* you can help. And then ask him *how*. Remember, he's having to deal with getting across roads all the time, so he's the best person to tell you what feels most secure and safe for him. You don't have to be skilled to help. And just because you don't know something, doesn't mean that you are – or that you're going to look – stupid.

Encouraging yourself to assist someone in this way is a very positive step in improving your self-esteem. For a start, helping a blind man might help you put your own problems in perspective. Yes, you have poor self-esteem, but you can do things to improve that. Whereas it's unlikely that the blind guy can do anything at all about the fact he's blind.

Very often it's nerve-wracking to walk up to someone and help him, but afterwards you'll feel a real sense of achievement. This is a good feeling, and I urge you to focus on it. You see, most people with poor self-esteem are not nearly in touch enough with their loving nature, or with the good things they do: they're far too busy dwelling on all their faults. So, allow yourself a chance to glow at your own goodness.

Also, congratulate yourself that you tackled something that – in some small way – drew attention to yourself. It may be that you go through life trying never to do this. Now you have. And the world didn't come to an end. The next time it'll be easier.

Scenario 2: The one about the students on the bus

This situation is more about speaking out. Some readers who can help a blind man cross the road, *can't* cope with using their voice to help someone.

If you have answered with a (b) or (c) it's quite likely that you would also avoid speaking in meetings, or even putting your point of view firmly across to friends, family, or a spouse.

Again, it's a good idea to encourage yourself to do it. If you take on the driver, you will feel a sense of pride that you can speak up for people unable to do so. You will also feel more in touch with your own core of goodness.

You might worry that your voice will sound timid, or that it might warble a bit with nerves, but it's unlikely that anyone else will notice.

Having a go – even if you feel tight with nerves – is highly likely to give you a buzz. This will encourage you on to even better things.

We all know that sinking feeling when we wish we'd intervened: when we know we should have helped or spoken out – but didn't. This feeling is very haunting. And it augments our belief that we're not capable, or brave, or worthy.

So, if you know that helping someone through speech is difficult – try this exercise:

Each day, try to smile and say 'hello' to five people you wouldn't normally speak to. If you're really shy this could feel like an impossible task. Agony, even! But after the first one or two it will get easier. And it will get you accustomed to using your voice – even when no one has spoken to you. You will also begin to find that being more outgoing brings rewards in that other people smile at you, or greet you more warmly. This will not only help you to feel better – your prevailing mood will be more cheerful – but you will also like yourself more. And that, as I've already said, is the key to better self-esteem.

Scenario 3: The one about being late for your doctor's appointment

If you answered (a) to this scenario, it means you are able to speak up on your own behalf – and also that:

- you can accept appropriate responsibility for your own lateness;
- you can accept criticism;
- you are able to work out a way that the situation might be saved and put that to someone else in a calm and assertive way.

So, anyone scoring (a) should give themselves a big pat on the back. Both (b) and (c) are unhealthy responses to this situation. If you chose (b) you probably already know that you tend to react crossly to embarrassing situations where you're in the wrong. The truth is that you're most cross with *you*, but that won't necessarily be apparent to anyone else who gets in your way!

If you answered (c), then you almost certainly use avoidance as a way of getting out of difficulties in life. Let's suppose, for example, you're asked to go out with your extended family to celebrate someone's birthday. And let's also suppose that this kind of gathering is your idea of total hell – but you don't feel able to say that. So, what are you likely to do? Probably, you'll simply fail to turn up. This will not endear you to your family!

And if you're asked to do something at work which you feel you can't do, you almost certainly won't ask for help, or explain that you're having difficulties, you just won't do it.

This kind of behaviour frequently leads to real trouble. People who are more confident find it difficult to believe that you're not being deliberately obstructive. They may even brand you as unreliable or a troublemaker. For you, however, anything is preferable to having to speak up on your own behalf.

But to return to the missed doctor's appointment. If you answered (c), I'm sure you know that by sloping off and not confronting this difficult situation you are not only being unfair to yourself, but also to the receptionist who is trying to manage the appointment system. Maybe you even feel guilty about it, but you still know that in real life you would have chosen to disappear.

Unfortunately, people who can't speak up for themselves, apologise, accept blame, or state their own case, tend to have real difficulties in work, with their families and in relationships.

But everyone can learn to be more open, more assertive and more effective with people – and you are no exception. In addition, as you gradually improve your estimation of yourself, you will find it's no longer such a big deal to face up to troublesome situations and to speak for yourself.

Scenario 4: The one about the school teacher

Again, (a) is the positive answer. You stick with what you know is right in terms of all the other demands being made on you – and you offer some help that fits in with that: in this case, buying and donating a few scones.

If you answered (b), you are falling into a very understandable, but common, trap. You are too busy trying to please everyone. This is very sweet – but it doesn't tend to help anyone else, least of all *you*. In fact, it creates pressure for you every single day of your life.

You also make the mistake of over-explaining. We all have a tendency to do this when we're unsure and nervous. All you need to say – firmly but with a smile – is: 'No, sorry. I'm too busy.' You don't have to explain yourself.

Try making a resolution from today that you'll be firmer with people and that you won't go into lengthy explanations when you have to say 'no'.

If you answered (c), then you're opening yourself up to even more stress.

The fact is that you cannot cram all these things into your Saturday. By saying 'yes' initially, you're only delaying the moment when you're going to have to say 'no'. That moment will come as soon as you discuss the weekend with your husband and family – who are probably going to be quite bewildered that you've even thought of compromising their 'important' arrangements. And then you're going to have to tell the teacher you can't help, which will be more upsetting for her than if you'd told her in the first place. And so you'll feel even more hopeless and distressed with yourself.

There will be more advice on using your voice effectively in Chapter Nine. But, meanwhile, remember just one thing: people with positive self-regard never say 'yes' when they want to say 'no'.

Scenario 5: The one about the sympathetic doctor

This situation can occur with all sorts of people – lawyers, lecturers, school teachers, bosses, politicians – as well as with doctors.

It happens when sympathy and consideration is shown to you by someone you don't know well – and usually by someone you are seeing in a professional capacity.

You may well have experienced something akin to the descriptions of feelings given in answers (b) and (c). I know I have at an earlier stage of my life when I had little self-value and my personal life was a disaster.

If you have answered (b) and you are in a close relationship, it is quite possible that you are not feeling sufficiently affirmed or loved *within* that relationship. This could be because you don't 'see' these loving signals. Or it could be that you are in a relationship that is draining you rather than buoying you up. Maybe this would be a good time to try to analyse just what is happening at home. I'll be returning to the whole question of self-esteem in relationships in Chapter Eleven.

You're more likely to have answered (c) if you're currently between relationships – and feeling quite bleak about it. At such times, it's very easy to daydream about love coming out of the blue from someone who is kind to you – in passing. Don't be ashamed of this. We've all done it. But it's not what tends to happen.

On the other hand, you want and need love – and you deserve it. And by working on your self-esteem, you are doing all you can to ensure that you attract someone suitable and lovely into your life.

Test three

These tests can be done over and over again – and I hope that as you progress through the book, you will find that your rating improves.

In every case, it's good and positive when you can put your mark as near as possible to the right-hand end where the rating is 100 per cent.

Readers who don't estimate themselves very highly will find it difficult to do that.

(a) Rate how worthwhile you are

Your instinct may be to put yourself down somewhere near 0 per cent. And perhaps you've done that. But now we're going to re-think it.

Who do you think was, or is, a really worthwhile person? Probably someone who acts kindly, makes people laugh, or who has great artistic ability. Perhaps someone who has achieved much against all the odds. I guess I would choose to put down someone like Nelson Mandela, but you may have your own very different ideas.

When you have chosen this paragon, decide on a percentage rating and then make a cross for him or her in the appropriate places on the line below. The chances are that this person will score pretty near the 100 per cent maximum.

0% **100%**

Next, come up with one or more names of people you think are – or were – much less worthwhile. These will probably be individuals you perceive to have behaved really badly in life. You might choose someone in your own family – especially if you were abused as a child. You could pick Hitler. Or a murderer, such as Ian Brady or the Yorkshire Ripper. When you have picked your people, decide on their ratings and make your crosses for them on the line – as near as you want to the minimum rating of 0 per cent.

Now decide on a rating for half a dozen other folk who feature in your life. For example: your boss, your mum or dad, your favourite teacher from your school days, your best friend, and someone you don't care for much.

Once you have awarded them a percentage rating, make an appropriate cross for each of them on the line.

Now you will have quite a lot of crosses for all these individuals on your line. Make sure, before you go any further, that you know which crosses signify which people – it's probably best to initial every cross that you've made.

Next I'd like you to check that you've put your cross for how worthwhile *you* are in the right place. Where should you *really* be placed on the line when you're compared with all these other men and women? Take some time over this. You'll almost certainly decide you want to adjust your place by moving it further to the right and nearer that magical figure of 100 per cent. I hope so.

Using a rating line – or continuum – is a very good way of making sure that you're thinking about yourself accurately, logically and appropriately.

I know it's hard work – and quite challenging – but please now repeat this procedure with all of the remaining sections of this test.

In each case, compare yourself as truthfully and accurately as you can with at least six other people, and then move your own rating accordingly.

(b) **Rate how lovable you are**
(c) **Rate how capable you are**
(d) **Rate how good a friend you are**

When you've had a go at this, you may find that it's been much easier for you to upgrade in some categories than in others.

For example, one of my clients – an attractive, charming and clever young woman – was able to improve all her ratings except the one about being capable. And yet she is a supremely capable person in a very high-powered job. However, her perception of herself at work is that she is not effective. This test has helped me to understand that this is an issue we need to focus on. After all, *I* can see that she's eminently capable – and so could you, if you met her – but *she* can't see herself that way, and that's what we must work on.

Don't worry if your ratings remain stubbornly low in some areas. Just carry on working at the rest of the book – and, from time to time, come back to these continuum tests and have another go at them.

By now – the end of Chapter Three – you have probably confirmed for yourself which areas of your life are most difficult. And you may have surprised yourself by getting low ratings in some sections where you didn't really know you had difficulties. But I hope you've also found that some bits of your life aren't as problematic as you'd feared.

At least now you should have a more comprehensive idea of what needs fixing. It may be that some of the suggestions I've made so far are getting you thinking more positively already.

In the next chapter we're going to look more closely at your childhood. This will complete the picture of who you are – and help you to understand why you think and behave as you do.

4

Where Did Your Habit of Poor Self-Esteem Come From?

Why do we need to look back?

We have to look back in order to understand where our bad habit of poor self-esteem came from. We weren't born with it. And we didn't catch it. We acquired it, because we didn't feel affirmed, loved, valued, or respected *enough*. And to find out why, we usually have to look at our upbringing.

The truth is that I've never met a person with poor self-esteem who had a mum and dad who were both really great at being parents.

On the other hand, most adults with positive self-esteem had loving and supportive parents.

When I was doing the research for this book, I interviewed a young woman doctor whom I'll call Catherine. She has fantastic self-esteem – and, not surprisingly, she had had wonderful parenting: the kind where you're told constantly that you're the most fabulous being on the planet. Catherine had had her problems, as we all have. One of these was being uprooted from one type of school to a completely different one at the opposite end of the country where the other children bullied her because she didn't know the things that they did and because she sounded different from them.

Catherine described all this to me, but it was clear that even though the bullying was unpleasant, it hadn't damaged her, or her perception of herself. The reason for this was that she continued to feel wanted and uniquely marvellous to her mum and dad. She had felt supported too. Because whenever she told her mother about the unkindness she was experiencing she was cuddled and comforted and told that the other children were 'just jealous'.

Catherine was given a golden start in life. But most people who have *poor* self-esteem were less lucky at home.

So your upbringing can't be ignored. But this chapter isn't just a hatchet job on your parents and an attempt to lay squarely on their shoulders all the blame for the problems you have today. In any event, 'blame' isn't a very helpful word – it only increases bitterness and bad feeling.

However, I believe that you'll gain some benefit if you examine what factors in your history may have damaged your self-esteem.

Now wouldn't it be great if by looking into your past you could magically transform yourself into a more contented, confident and assertive *you*?

If real life were like an episode of *Star Trek*, you'd probably read this chapter, see a flash of light, fall into a faint, and then wake up with such amazing new insight that the rest of your life would be a breeze!

I wish I could promise to make such a dramatic difference. I can't. But what I *can* do is to help you to identify likely problems of the past and to connect them to your current difficulties. Knowing that there's a reason why life is tough often makes it less tough. So although the harsh truth is that you can't change the past, the great news is that you *can* change how you view it – and how you consequently view yourself. In other words, we're certainly not going to dwell on the past – we're going to deal with it and move on.

It is entirely possible that you don't really want to delve into your background. You may be fearful of what you'll find. Or perhaps you worry that stirring up the past will make you feel even worse. Or maybe you don't think your childhood is relevant: plenty of people reckon that their childhoods were 'OK', and not responsible for their current feelings.

Let me just say that many sufferers of the poor self-esteem habit had the sort of upbringing that appeared unremarkable and normal – at least from the outside. You don't need to have had a violent, drunken parent, or to have been abandoned in childhood, to have a poor sense of self-value. Far more commonly, bad self-esteem habits originate in childhoods where the parents did nothing specifically *wrong*: it's just that they never did anything specifically *right* – or they just didn't do enough. In other words, it's what they *didn't* do that caused the problems, not what they *did*.

Often, when I ask someone about their childhood, they will preface their remarks by saying: 'I bet all your other clients had worse childhoods than I had. I shouldn't complain . . . I was fed and clothed . . .'

In other words, most people feel protective about their parents to some extent – and they also feel guilty about criticising them. But I'm not interested in whether this client had a worse time than that one. It's not a competition! All I'm interested in is providing an atmosphere where any client can get anything about anyone off his or her chest – and can feel that it's safe to do so within the four walls of my consulting room.

Now, I don't know specifically what it is in your past that has hindered your appreciation of yourself, but I hope that by reading about some typical examples of not very helpful parenting, you will gain some helpful insight into why you don't value yourself as much as you could.

There's another compelling reason why you should sort out your feelings about your mother and/or father, which is that most of our parents are going to be around for a very long time. It's not unusual these days to still have both parents when you are well into mid-life – and you may even be quite elderly before you are orphaned. This is a great bonus for all those individuals who received warm, uncomplicated, authentic and affirming love from their mums and dads –

and who are able to feel these things in return. But, for the many of us who have more mixed feelings about our parenting, the picture is less rosy.

If you feel that you were never sufficiently loved as a child, or that you were constantly ridiculed, criticised or ignored, then you will tend to feel resentful of ageing parents who gradually make more and more demands on your time, your attention and your emotions.

You may be struggling with your own career, or relationship, or your children – and not feeling very confident about any of them. In these circumstances, the added burden of a dependent parent can feel like a pressure too far. You may even find yourself wishing that your parents would die. And you'll almost certainly yearn for some quality time on earth – before you're too old to enjoy it – without having to consider the needs of the older generation.

A friend of mine, whose parents have never been emotionally available to her, confided: 'I don't actually want my mother and father to die – so long as they're still having a reasonable time – but I do wish that their lives were nothing to do with me.'

What can you do if you're in this kind of situation? One way of dealing with it is to fully acknowledge what was right and what was wrong with your upbringing and try to come to terms with it. Then – with this knowledge – you are in a better position to assess for yourself just how available you feel you can be to your parents. This may sound very calculated, but if you don't think this out, you'll always be in danger of denying your own rights as a worthwhile person. You'll also feel increasingly pressurised.

My belief is that no one can expect a huge amount of love or support from their kids if they never dished it out in the first place. You get back what you put out.

Of course, many people who are more emotionally mature than their own parents have learned how to be openly kind and compassionate – and they do try to give their parents more than they received. But in order to stay mentally healthy they need to set their own limits of just how much they're prepared to do and to give.

If they try to give too much, they become resentful. Sometimes they even become ill. Kindness is one of the world's most vital emotions – but we all need to be kind to ourselves, as well as to other people.

The fact is that each family must find its own solutions to the ageing parent situation. We have to learn to make it work in our own way.

There may be all sorts of moral blackmail exerted on you by other relatives, or even by your parents' neighbours, but these individuals don't know the dynamics of your particular set up – and they have no idea what went on behind closed doors when you were a child.

People with little regard for themselves find it very hard to deal with family demands on them, but if they are to feel happier and more assertive, and more in charge of their own lives, this is one area that they really have to sort. If they don't, they'll always feel swamped by others. They'll also be in danger of growing old without ever putting a premium on their own needs and wants: something that is necessary if they're to develop appropriate regard for themselves.

How might you feel as you examine your past and your parenting?

Just before you look at the different types of parents characterised below, one word of warning. Just like a medical student who worries that he's got every disease that he studies, you might feel that there are elements of all the following parental-types in your family situation. That is OK. Quite often, there's some overlap between the various categories.

You might also feel extraordinarily angry. Or you might feel very sad, or full of longing, as you accept that you were short-changed in the parenting stakes. That is normal too.

The important thing here is for you to use this chapter to reappraise your relationship with your parents, and then to formulate where that relationship is going in the future.

Once you've accepted what they were really like – with all the sense of anger or sorrow that that might entail – you will move on to looking at their situation more objectively. In fact, you'll almost certainly come to a point where you can understand what made them the parents that they were – even if you can't totally forgive them for their flaws, or forget their weaknesses.

We humans have an amazing capacity for loving kindness, and you'll probably find this bubbling up in you. But – and this is the key point – these newer, more tender emotions don't tend to present themselves till you've really let yourself see and feel the worst of what happened to you as a child.

As I mentioned earlier in the book, while you work on understanding your past – and you struggle with the concept of valuing yourself more – you will find that you develop more time and more understanding for others.

For a start, individuals to whom you may have felt inferior, will seem more human. They may still seem confident, clever, attractive or whatever, but you'll begin to gain some sense of what it's cost them to become this 'whole' person.

As for people you have had difficulties with, you will feel more keenly than ever before that they too have a right to be here, and a right to make mistakes.

This insight into other people is particularly helpful when it happens within your family circle. In the very week that I'm writing this chapter, one of my clients – whom I'll call Clara – has just started to forge a new relationship with her mother: a woman who has been difficult to deal with in the past.

The truth is that Clara's mother had been very miserable for years, but reluctant to do anything about it. She also tried to lean on her children and couldn't understand it if they were unable to cope with her. As a result, Clara had been avoiding her for ages.

But, as Clara and I worked together, and as she took responsibility for gaining a new habit of good self-esteem – and faced up to the difficulties of her childhood – she began to blossom.

This week she was happy to tell me that she has had several very emotional conversations with her mother where she has felt able to speak about their difficult relationship. Having opened this dialogue, she has begun to feel more genuine fondness for her parent than she has for years. This fondness – which has taken her a bit by surprise – is a completely different feeling from the one she has lived with for so long, which was much more about hating her mother, but feeling that she 'ought' to love her.

An even greater bonus has been that Clara's mum has been so delighted by her daughter's increased contentment, openness and assurance, that she has agreed to get some professional help with her *own* problems. This – as you can imagine – is quite a weight off Clara, who always felt that she was expected to somehow try to make her mother's life better: a task that seemed so impossible it compounded her difficulties with her parent and reinforced her own feelings of failure.

Not everyone who faces up to their parenting and develops a good self-esteem habit enjoys quite the success that Clara has experienced. But many do. And you could be among them.

As you go through this chapter, don't worry if you're angry. If you feel angry – it's almost certainly justifiable. And don't worry if you're sad – that's natural. Just remember that you're going through phases of recognition of what really happened in your house. This recognition and acceptance will endow you with greater understanding of the past. And this in turn will help you to put your childhood into a better perspective. Once you've done this, you'll find that you'll move forward with more positive self-regard and confidence.

Your way of going forward may involve you challenging a parent over harsh, or unfair, or unloving treatment.

Your way of going forward may be to feel more love for a parent who has been too emotionally timid to live life fully, or to be demonstrative.

Your way of going forward may be to accept that you and your parents are very different people. Not worse. Not better. Just different.

Your way of going forward may be to reappraise how much contact you want with them – more or less – from now on.

What if your parents are already dead?

If your parents are already dead, is there much point in looking back on your childhood and trying to sort it?

Yes, there is. It can still help to fully accept the type of upbringing you had, and to see for yourself what factors in it may have led to a habit of poor self-esteem.

But, having glanced back in time, what can you do with any new feelings that arise when you're not able to discuss it with your parents?

Here are a few suggestions:

Talk with your siblings

First of all, unless you are an only child, there's a strong possibility that your feelings about your late parents will not be so very different from at least one of your siblings.

I have a client whose mother died recently – and she and her brother have had a few late-night sessions comparing notes about their upbringings, and about their feelings for their dead parent. Each of them is gaining a fresh perspective on their mother, who is becoming even more real and more complete to them as a result. Try to share what you're going through with a brother or sister.

Have an 'empty-chair' conversation

This is a technique that was devised by the founder of a school of psychotherapy called Gestalt. It's used by many therapists during sessions, but you can try it on your own and see if it helps.

What you do is to sit in a quiet room opposite an empty chair. In that chair you – mentally – place the dead parent you want to talk to. You can imagine him as a young person, or as your elderly parent, or even as the spirit of the deceased. And you then speak aloud and tell this 'being' everything you want to get off your chest.

You might find yourself crying, or asking questions, or raising your voice angrily. This exercise does tend to loosen up a load of buttoned-up emotions that have been weighing you down.

After you've put your questions and told this parent things you never got round to telling them in life – good or bad – you can swap chairs. You then become the parent. And, as your parent, you talk to 'you' in the opposite empty chair and try to answer the questions and the accusations that have been raised. You try to make sense of things from your dead parent's point of view. You can explain yourself, apologise, and express love in a way that the real parent may never have managed to do.

You can swap chairs again and, as yourself, comment on what's been said. Indeed you can keep the dialogue going for ages. But my advice is not to let it go on for longer than about half an hour. And if, by any chance, this exercise raises big questions for you, or seems to bring out such sad or angry feelings that you feel overwhelmed by them, then do get some bereavement counselling as a matter of urgency. Useful details can be found in the Help Yourself Guide.

Make a pictorial record

Having done some thinking about one or other of your parents, you might find that you'd like to concentrate on some positive aspects of them, so that although you've acknowledged all was not well with the relationship, you choose to remember the good times more than the bad.

One way of doing this is to make a pictorial record. By collecting together pictures of earlier – and hopefully happier – times, you will find yourself focusing on a rather more palatable image of your dead parent. This will be especially valuable if a parent's last days were a living nightmare: perhaps he or she was in excruciating pain, or moody, or angry, or even so drugged-up that they didn't know what was happening, or who you were.

This kind of end is very sad for everyone – and it can leave you with a very skewed and unpleasant memory of your parent, which has little to do with the feelings you had for each other in more normal times.

Collect together all the photographs that show the family at its happiest. You might want to collate all this into one album – and maybe even add to it some written recollections of good times.

Write a letter

You may feel very angry and upset with a dead parent – particularly one who you feel never loved you enough.

One way of dealing with this is to write your parent a letter – a letter that might take weeks to write. Put it all down – every last sad thought or accusation.

This in itself will liberate your mind. And then you can either keep the letter somewhere safe – and refer back to it from time to time – or destroy it. Frequently, people do feel that having had their final, uninterrupted say, they can 'let go' of all of their unresolved feelings. Some individuals make some kind of private ceremony of the process where they burn the letter, or bury it in the garden. Others prefer just to put it out with the rubbish. I'm sure you'll decide on what feels right for you.

Arrange some sort of memorial

Having come to terms with who and what your mum and dad were – whether they were good, bad, or, as in most cases, variable parents – it might help to have some kind of memorial to them. By formalising their memory you'll be able to arrive at some 'closing' thought or statement, such as: 'You weren't perfect parents, but there were reasons for that, and there was love between us, which lives on in me.'

Even if you still have feelings of hostility towards your parents, making a memorial to them can help you draw a line under the past – and to go forward into your future.

Your memorial can be something very simple, such as a rose tree, or a window box. It can be a prize donated in their name at an organisation they loved, such as the local cricket club. Or it might be a financial gift to a cause they believed in. It could even be a bench in the park.

Whatever it is, it should help you to feel that you have dealt with the memory of your dead parents as well as you can, and that you have formally marked their passing.

Parenting that contributes to low self-esteem

We turn now to parents who are still alive. Many of them will fall into at least one of the following six categories:

1 Critical Parents (CPs)

Parents fitting this type are most likely to say:

- you're stupid;
- you didn't make the team because you don't train hard enough;
- why can't you be more like your sister/mother/dad etc?;
- you never were any good at relationships;
- aren't you too plump for that skirt?;
- 95 per cent isn't good enough – you should have got 100 per cent.

And they're least likely to say:

- Well done, you did your best;
- Sweetheart, you look gorgeous.

Living with CPs is very hard work. The truth is that you can rarely please them. Sometimes they actually love you very much indeed – it's just that they're not good at showing it. They want the best for you – or maybe they really want the best for themselves! As a result, they are likely to push you so that you achieve – be it academically, in sport, the arts, or financially and socially.

What is tough to deal with is the hideous sense of inevitability that you'll never come up to scratch. And when, even in adult life, you hope that this kind of parent will take your side when your marriage breaks up – or you lose your job – you will almost certainly be disappointed, yet again.

The CP may criticise you about your lack of achievements or performance, or about how you look. Sometimes they criticise everything – sometimes they're more specific.

It's very common for a man who is keen on sport and 'manly pursuits' to be intensely critical of a son who doesn't have those interests – whereas he may not nag about school work, or even notice if the boy excels in the classroom. Frequently, such a son is left with a massive sense of inferiority about his body and his co-ordination and masculinity. He is often also very, very angry about his father's jibes and put-downs – even if he keeps this to himself.

There's another type of CP who, I believe, does genuinely love his or her children, but who spoils pleasurable moments by a type of criticism which masquerades as concern.

Laura's mother falls into this category.

Laura has a high-powered sales job with a telecommunications company. This involves her driving up and down the country, giving sales presentations. She suspects that – despite her healthy salary – she is something of a disappointment to her mother: she isn't an academic success like her brothers, neither has she, as yet, produced the longed-for grandchild. But her mother never expresses these disappointments or criticisms directly. Instead, she makes worrying noises at the danger Laura is in.

'Oh dear,' her mother will say, 'you've got to drive to Aberdeen. That's a long way. You're bound to have an accident if you keep driving these long distances . . . I mean, it must increase your chances . . . you're always on the road . . . you must get tired . . .'

Laura's mother's comments are not helpful: they sow a seed of fear in Laura's mind, which niggles away all the time she's at the wheel. And so, where she should be able to enjoy a few hours driving – and be able to mentally prepare herself for a big sales meeting – she feels anxious and nervy, and is likely to end up with a headache.

'I do know that she loves me,' says Laura. 'But I also know that her "concern" is not really about my health and well-being, it's about her misgivings concerning my lifestyle. She can't see why I do what I do – and also why I don't have the perfect boyfriend. These things seem to be an affront to my mother. The end result, of course, is that I tell her less and less about my life – because I'm fed up with dealing with her anxiety, and I'm sick and tired of trying to justify myself and my achievements.'

Like Laura, many children of CPs achieve a great deal in life – though they tend to feel that whatever they do, it's not enough.

Unfortunately, some offspring of CPs decide that since they're never going to be able to fulfil all expectations of them, they will 'drop out' and do as little as possible.

So the legacy of this kind of parenting tends to be that you feel:

- stupid;
- lazy;
- feeble;
- unattractive;
- bound to fail.

These feelings are damaging. So if *you* had this kind of upbringing, how can you get over it?

It usually helps to try to spare a thought for what turned your parent into this demanding, driven and – perhaps – bitter person.

Perhaps your parent was brought up that way? On the other hand, perhaps he or she came from a pretty hopeless background where no one achieved anything – or where there was alcoholism, or real poverty?

Gaining some sort of understanding of the reason behind all the criticism may help you. But you should also be able to recognise that, much as there may have been extenuating circumstances for your CP's behaviour, you still have a right to feel angry or saddened by it.

In the next chapter we'll be looking at the kind of Negative Inner Commentary that you're likely to have been left with, and how to replace that with better feelings about yourself.

Remember: insight brings understanding. And understanding paves the way for change.

Try saying: 'Yes, now I can see why I so often feel really stupid, or unattractive, or ineffectual. It's obviously not my fault, so I'm going to stop blaming myself for it.'

If you can accept this statement and learn to 'own' it, you'll have taken a positive step towards increasing your sense of self-worth.

2 Squabbling Parents (SPs)

With parents like yours, you probably felt as if World War Three was likely to erupt at any moment.

There are few more terrifying sights or sounds to a child than a quarrel between his parents. If you grew up in an atmosphere where there were lots of rows, this will almost certainly have had an impact on your self-esteem.

For a start, when parents quarrel, we tend to feel that we're not noticed. Or that we're not important enough. Or that we're not interesting enough to distract them from their battleground.

Often, too – unfortunately – at least one child in the family gets singled out to be fought over. Perhaps you know what it was like to be favoured by dad – and to have your mother berate him for making time for you, but not for others in the family?

This kind of scene is never the child's fault. But it feels as if it is at the time.

SPs are most likely to say to you:

- 'If you take Mum's side, I won't talk to you.'
- 'Don't interrupt when we're arguing.'
- 'Shut up – and go to your room.'
- 'I'm leaving – then you'll be sorry!'

And they're least likely to say:

- 'Let's not get overheated – we'll all sit down and have a chat about this round the kitchen table.'

Adults who grew up in this kind of emotional war zone can easily turn into very angry people themselves – we do, after all, learn by imitation. They frequently shout at their own children, even though they hate themselves when they do so.

It takes a lot of effort to break out of the example you've been given – where shouting and arguments are the order of the day – and to change into someone who calmly discusses differences of opinion.

Some offspring of SPs become loners. To them families spell trouble, and they believe that relationships are bound to end in pain. Many such individuals become very controlled and do their utmost to avoid excessive emotions. So while they save themselves from pain, they frequently miss out on life's happier moments as well. This is one form of survival – and an understandable one. But it can result in quite a solitary existence.

If you tend to keep yourself to yourself – and you know that you have kept a tight rein on your emotions in order to avoid becoming anything like your parents – this book may encourage you to the view that you can risk more in life.

Don't forget: you don't have to be a replica of your mum or dad. Neither do you have to be an emotional recluse. You can be something in between. Of course you have their genes buzzing around inside you, but you are also uniquely yourself – with your own characteristics and your own free will.

Other individuals whose parents fought all the time, *do* form relationships but tend to feel insecure within them. They become very upset by the manifestation of any difference of opinion with a partner, and if they suspect their partner is actually angry, they feel threatened and terrified. So much so that instead of talking about any disagreements, this type of person will avoid any discussion – in case it proves dangerous and makes things worse – and will physically retreat to take a bath, or weed the garden, or go down to the pub.

If this all sounds like you – and what you've been through – the chances are that you often feel:

- terrified of anger;
- unwanted;
- helpless;
- vulnerable.

In order to start trying to tackle these feelings that probably bother you much of the time, try to work out for yourself what your SPs were so angry about – and why they acted as they did. In many homes, the man is less articulate than the woman, and when she wins verbal arguments he gets furiously angry – even to the point of violence. Did this happen in your house? If so, can you feel some small sense of sorrow for your father in his frustration?

Was your mother perhaps jealous of you? Was this about her lack of confidence or self-esteem? Can you find it in your heart to face up to the painful feelings you have about her, but also to acknowledge that there were probably reasons for her own insecurities?

Perhaps thinking back to how she was can help make you more determined to stop the rot. Your mother may never have tried to change, but you can. You can resolve to be different, to learn to deal with your problems, and to emerge as a stronger person who can argue her case without fighting.

Were your parents passionately in love – even though they fought like cat and dog? Were they, perhaps, two very needy people who could never quite give each other the attention and the overwhelming love that each of them craved?

Can you understand those feelings? Perhaps you've had them yourself?

Unlike your mother and father, you are now working on becoming responsible for your own core of happiness and your own sense of self-worth. By developing yourself in this way, you'll be able to avoid the pitfalls that your parents fell into.

As I've said before, when a person requires another person to *make* him or her happy – and demands that any partner must be totally devoted and faithful and caring – then that person is always going to end up disappointed, or is going to go through life terrified that disappointment is just around the corner.

To alleviate this torment – because that is what it is – we need to accept that our sense of self, and our inner core of happiness, are *our own* responsibility, and no one else's. When we embrace this concept, we will find loving partners to enhance our good feelings, but we won't demand that they 'make us happy'.

3 Timid, Undemonstrative Parents (TUPs)

Now we come to the third category of problem parents – the TUPs. These are the sort of parents who seem fine from outside the house, but who are a nightmare inside it.

They are most likely to say:

- Don't show off.
- Don't show me up.
- Don't exaggerate.
- Well, I don't see how we can help you, but we won't stand in your way . . .

They are least likely to say:

- You're so brilliant.
- You look fantastic.
- Let me pick up the phone and see if I can get you that interview.
- So you want to be a pop star/actress/astronaut? Go for it – you're so wonderful, you're bound to succeed.

TUPs don't tend to be seriously bad parents but they don't ever 'give' enough to be effective ones either.

The truth is that they don't contribute much to life. Their timidity means that they err on the side of caution. They don't take risks, so they never shine in their chosen careers. They don't usually excel with their hobbies either – and they rarely have many friends.

Quite commonly, they will take their holidays in the same place year after year. And they will seldom challenge the views, politics or religion that they were brought up with. In fact, they are most reluctant to even begin to examine their inner thoughts and what makes them tick – probably because they are terrified of the disruption it would cause. For this reason, TUPs tend to avoid marital counselling, support groups and therapy in general.

TUPs don't allow themselves to feel very expansive emotions. If – when they appear to be very fit and well – you ask them how they are, they'll answer: 'Pretty fair.'

And if you suggest taking them out to celebrate their wedding anniversary, they'll probably answer: 'Um – yes, I *think* we're free on that day.'

You may still, even now, long for them to break out of this constraint. You may still hope they'll say: 'Terrific', when you ask how they are. Or that they'll enthuse about your suggestion of an outing by saying: 'What a marvellous treat. How lovely. You have such great ideas.'

Stop hoping – because you're always going to be disappointed!

The best you can say about TUPs is that they don't usually complain when they hit hard times or become ill. 'Mustn't grumble,' they say. Or: 'I'm sure other people are much worse off than we are.'

Some people think that the TUPs are the salt of the earth. And that they represent the best of everything that is British.

Personally, I disagree. Their attitude is depressing and frequently leaves a trail of wreckage in its wake.

One of their worst traits is a tendency to make jokes at their own children's expense – especially when other people are praising them. They do this because they're embarrassed and ill at ease socially. But their particular brand of humour can devastate their offspring.

So, the ballet teacher may praise little Linda's hard work and artistry but her TUP will be unable to say: 'Thanks very much. Yes, we're enormously proud of her.' Instead, a likely response will be: 'Suppose she's not bad for someone who's got flat feet and no sense of rhythm.'

Or a family friend may be very impressed with ten-year-old Jonathan's football skills. But can the TUP enjoy the approbation? No. Instead, he or she will say: 'He got lucky today.' Or: 'Not exactly David Beckham, though, is he?'

These comments can echo round the brain of their children for the rest of their lives.

Another way in which the TUPs are damaging to their children is in their attitude to love, sex and tactile warmth.

Often TUPs have difficult relationships and sex lives – simply because of their timidity and stunted emotions. So their offspring are not given very positive messages about close, intimate loving.

Frequently, TUPs aren't very comfortable with their own children's desire for closeness. A TUP may avoid bouncing her own child on her knee, and may well look embarrassed when her own child runs to her at the school gate and yells: ' I love you, Mummy.'

As if that weren't bad enough, children of TUPs can't expect much back-up if they're picked on by a teacher, or by pupils, at school. The TUP will say, rather helplessly: 'I'm sure it's not as bad as you say.' Or: 'Well, what had you done to her?' Or: 'Just tell her that it's naughty to bully people.'

The effect of the TUPs' behaviour on their children is usually to alienate them. Because when a child is let down on important and worrying issues, and is never affirmed – either for his or her looks or ability – and is rarely hugged, the only way to survive is to depend on him or herself.

Vast numbers of people who have poor self-esteem were brought up by TUPs. They frequently feel that they were given no help or support in childhood and that their talents were never recognised. They also feel 'average' – at best – because no one ever told them how special they were. Many of them feel incredibly sad that they didn't have more affirming parenting, and that they never had real family closeness of the kind that many other folk take for granted.

They also tend to feel guilty – because they know that TUPs aren't the worst people in the world, and that other people have had far more violent or deprived childhoods.

If this sounds like you, you need to take on board that being the child of a TUP gives you a very poor start in the self-esteem stakes – and that your guilt is out of place.

Because of your TUP upbringing, you have a big emotional hill to climb if you are to feel worthwhile and interesting – but you can do it.

Children of TUPs often feel:

- unlovable;
- unwanted;
- unattractive;
- undesirable;
- unworthy;
- not respected;
- stupid.

These are very inhibiting feelings, but it's important to realise that although your parents – in their timidity and lack of connection with the real world – imbued you with all these negative emotions, you *can* develop positive ones to take their place. It's also important to realise that feelings about yourself can be entirely false. In other words, just because you feel something very strongly about yourself, it doesn't necessarily mean it must be true.

So, one way of dealing with having TUPs as parents is to challenge your beliefs and thoughts about yourself. This will help you to develop a new habit of positive self-regard.

And what of the TUPs themselves – particularly as they grow older?

If you are working to develop your own life and your own sense of being valid and special, you may well feel that you can't spend too much time with your parents – because being with them drags you down again.

Your feelings are justified – and you should try not to feel guilty about them. Only you know what a struggle you've had – or are having – to forge your own way in life. If you don't feel you've got much spare energy for your parents, then that, I'm afraid, is what they have brought on themselves – albeit unwittingly.

Having said that, TUPs are not evil parents. And if we can find it in our hearts to spend some time with them, and to try and offer them more affirmation and love than we feel they gave us, we can feel proud of ourselves. And this feeling of pride will foster our own sense of our kindness and goodness – which is very important in the development of a good self-esteem habit.

But – and this is a vital point – we won't experience these good feelings if we allow ourselves to be pressurised into having much more contact with our TUPs than we can comfortably deal with. So it's up to you to decide for yourself how much contact you can offer your parents at this time in your life. You can review the situation as often as you like – but ultimately it must be your decision.

4 Parents Who Only Notice 'Naughty' Children (PWONNCs)

These parents are frequently immature, and not ready for parent-hood. They may have all sorts of problems themselves – including mental illness or alcoholism – and though they often do truly love their children, they don't seem to be able to put much effort into looking after them.

They are most likely to say:

- You never give me a moment's peace.
- You're a bad, wicked child.
- You get on my nerves.
- You're ruining everything for me.
- You were such a difficult child.

And they're least likely to say:

- You are a really lovely child and I love you very, very much, but your behaviour today is disappointing.
- How lovely to see you reading quietly. What a good boy/girl you are.
- I'm sorry, love, I've not paid you any attention today. Let's play something for half an hour – just you and me.
- You are/were such a lovely child.

Wise parents always try to love and affirm their children, even if they sometimes have to criticise their behaviour. They know that when youngsters are constantly told that they're 'horrible', 'infuriating', 'ugly', or a 'menace', these labels stick with them through life.

However, this concept of criticising behaviour as opposed to criticising the child is, alas, usually far beyond the emotional intelligence of this type of parent.

Many PWONNCs didn't have great childhoods themselves – but that fact doesn't help their children.

It's quite common for PWONNCs to have several different partners in their quest to find true love – and to have children by all of them. What tends to happen is that the children of the latest relationship – or the one that has gone best – are favoured by the parent, while the other youngsters are left out in the emotional cold.

I can remember taking a call on a television programme from just such a parent. The caller was a woman in her thirties, and she had rung in for advice on how to deal with her nine-year-old son who was 'doing her head in'.

It turned out that this son's father had walked out years ago, and the guy who replaced him – and who had tried to be a good stepfather – had been dumped.

Now there was a new man in the house – and this time, according to my caller, she had found 'real love' and they were actively trying for another baby.

Her life would have been perfect, she told me, had it not been for her son being such a bad boy.

I hardly knew where to begin. What was screamingly obvious was that the 'difficult' nine-year-old was a very confused little boy who had no idea whether he was loved or not – and by whom.

So, what did he do? He made a thorough nuisance of himself. And why? Because if he played quietly, or got absorbed in watching television, he became invisible to his mum.

Such children quickly decide that it's better to get some reaction – even if it's one of exasperation – than none at all.

It's so painful to think of children who are reduced to behaving badly just to get noticed. The child of that caller was definitely an example of that. I like to think that some of the points I made to that mother possibly changed her attitude and opened her eyes to what she was doing to the child she already had – while she was so busy trying for another one. I'm not optimistic, however.

Perhaps you can identify with this kind of upbringing – where you never got noticed unless you stepped out of line? If so, I am very sorry because your journey to find greater self-esteem is likely to be a tough one.

It often helps to look at your parents as a product of their own parenting, and also to look at their immaturity, or personality problems. Sometimes this can help you to understand their apparent callousness.

However, the most important thing you can do is to re-evaluate yourself according to what more rational people in your life think of you. Yes, you had a lousy beginning, and yes, you doubtless received negative messages about yourself – but you don't have to believe them.

Is it very likely that your parents – who clearly lacked insight, and who weren't very adequate as people, let alone as parents – were a good judge of you? Or of anything else, for that matter? Probably not. So I doubt that there is much evidence for their criticism of you. Their hurtful comments and abrasive behaviour do not mean that you are a horrible or worthless person. Not at all.

Often the children of PWONNCs had an aunt or a granny who really loved them and who gave out positive messages of affirmation. Did you? If so, try to focus on the fact that this other person – probably a much more organised, whole and perceptive person than your parents – loved you a lot, and valued you very highly.

Allow yourself to remember how special that felt. There will have been other people in your life who have shown you how valuable you are. A school teacher, perhaps; a friend; a partner; or a child of your own.

Listen to the messages you've got from people like these.

A wonderful character called Barbara Woodhouse – who trained dogs on television in the 1970s and 1980s – used to say that there was no such thing as a bad dog, only bad owners. I'm sure the same can be said of children and parents!

You weren't bad, or horrible, or worthless – even if your behaviour left much to be desired. And it's not your fault that you had a PWONNC for a parent. You were just trying to get the attention that a child has a right to expect.

5 The Self-Centred Parent (SCP)

The fifth category is the self-centred parent, who basically judges everything in life by how it affects him or her.

All sorts of people can come into this category: immature parents, neurotic parents, depressed parents and just very inward-looking or selfish parents.

Obviously, some of these people are actually ill, and are therefore not wholly responsible for their poor parenting skills. But, unfortunately, the effect of a SCP on kids – whatever the reason for it – can be quite devastating.

They are most likely to say:

- Mummy's busy.
- What have *you* got to worry about? I'm the one with the real problems.
- No, you can't have a party – I'm not well enough for all that noise.
- I've got a headache – go away.
- You can't possibly be ill today – why are you doing this to me?

They are least likely to say:

- Please, tell me all about your day.
- I'll help you with your homework.
- You look a bit upset – did you have a bad time at school?

SCPs can be charming – when it suits them. They like to be the centre of attention, so if you have a group of friends round, your SCP will take the floor and chat away, and show great interest in the activities of all of your mates. This may well leave you feeling very uninteresting. You may also feel angry because you could do with similar interest being shown to you. Also, you may feel that you can no longer complain about your SCP to your mates – because they now appear to think that your SCP is fun and fascinating.

This kind of SCP will try to get you into the best schools, or university, but you'll always have a sneaking feeling that this is more about their kudos than your academic benefit.

Theatrical mums come into this category – and they can be mothers from hell! They keep urging their kids on to get theatre or film parts or commercials in an attempt to live a more exciting life themselves. Woe betide you if you don't *want* this theatrical career, or you're not very good at it. Your SCP will hold this against you for ever.

Many SCPs, however, are so busy with their own lives and careers that they have little interest in pushing you: they just don't want you to get in the way.

The daughter of a famous writer once told me that her mother never, ever stopped writing to welcome her home from school – even when she was little. On one level she understood that her mother wrote for a living and that they had a comfortable life because of it, but on another level she felt rejected and uninteresting. As an adult, this writer's daughter finds it hard to understand why her mother could not have taken a break for just ten minutes each afternoon, just to have a quick chat with her own child.

Many SCPs occasionally have a surge of guilt that they don't give you enough attention and will buy you a present. The trouble is that this present is frequently something you don't actually want – and is a further demonstration that your SCP doesn't actually know you, or know what you like.

Of course, an SCP who is depressed is rather different. He or she will command attention in a completely different way from more flamboyant SCPs. This is likely to be in ways that prevent you from doing things. You won't be able to have friends round, perhaps – or to make a noise. And you won't be able to rely on your SCP coming to a parent-teacher meeting, or turning up to see you play hockey.

Unfortunately, your parent's sadness will have the effect of cutting him or her off from you. It must be stressed that this behaviour is often beyond a depressed person's control, but it does leave you with a feeling that your parent is not available to you – and that's a very lonely feeling for a child, and one that can engender feelings of unworthiness.

SCPs also tend to look as if they're withdrawing love from you if you disappoint or anger them in any way.

One client of mine described how her mother's anger was terrifying:

'She was a hairdresser – and we lived above her shop. If I made too much noise, she would come tearing up the stairs to the flat and her eyes were like pools of hatred. I couldn't believe the hostility that was being directed against me. I know I was noisy sometimes, but when she looked at me there was no love in her expression, just hate. It meant that when she came up after work and then demanded that I: "Kiss Mummy", I didn't want to. I withdrew from her, I suppose. She made me feel I was hateful.'

This is a very common feeling among children of SCPs. They are most likely to feel that they are:

- uninteresting;
- in the way;
- annoying;
- unlovable;
- unwanted;
- they must please people and not cause any trouble.

What can you do if you're an adult who was brought up by a SCP? Try to realise that your parent wouldn't have been available to *any* child, no matter how utterly fantastic that child was. SCPs are selfish. Their only view of life is one based on how any situation affects them.

If your SCP was actually funny and engaging, you might find that as an adult you are able to spend time together, so long as you never get on to any important issues.

But as SCPs get older, they always feel that you *ought* to do more for them. It's very important in order to maintain your own space and self-esteem that you set firm parameters on this involvement. You had a childhood where you played a supporting role to your parent. Do you always want to be a bit part player in their life? Or would you like to star in your own?

As I've said elsewhere in this chapter, kindness to a parent can often help us to feel better about ourselves and to heal rifts. But an SCP will always make more and more demands on you. For your own sense of self-worth you should strive to make a decision about how much contact with your SCP is healthy for *you*. It's your turn now and you need to put yourself first.

It's likely that for as long as he or she lives, your SCP will have the capacity to upset your equilibrium so that you feel like an unsure child all over again.

You can stop this happening. You don't have to go down that road. You are a special, worthwhile person. Don't let anyone else's behaviour or attitude rid you of that belief.

6 The Utterly Different From You Parents (UDFYPs)

Sometimes a child grows up feeling that he or she is very different from everyone else in the house – especially one or other of the grown-ups.

It happens when temperament is markedly different, or when the young person's interests are in complete contrast to that of his parents. It can also occur when a child is physically different from one or other parent.

The UDFYP is most likely to say:

- You're a complete mystery to me.
- You're odd.
- You're ungrateful.

And least likely to say:

- I know exactly how you feel.
- You're *so* like me.

As I've said earlier in the book, sometimes there's a biological reason for these differences in that the man of the house may be bringing up another man's child – knowingly or unknowingly. Many individuals actually feel they can make sense of these differences if they find out later that the people they thought were their birth parents actually weren't.

I remember interviewing Anita Roddick – founder of The Body Shop – a few years ago. She spoke very movingly of her joy at discovering who her 'real' father was – and how that helped her make sense of who *she* was, and gave her more of a sense of belonging.

UDFYPs can be critical, like CPs, or have characteristics of many of the other types listed above, but the main feature of their parenting is that they find you bewildering. This tends to make them hostile.

Many gay adults have UDFYPs. They often sensed that at least one parent disapproved of them – frequently from way back in early childhood. They felt different, and they were aware that their mother or father also sensed this difference and were profoundly uncomfortable and embarrassed about it.

Nowadays, there is another significant group of young adults who feel that there are enormous differences between them and their parents. These are individuals who were born and educated in the UK and who have an eclectic mix of friends, but whose parents were immigrants who have maintained the culture and traditions of their home country.

I have a client whom I'll call Jaspal. She's a brilliant young woman who's a qualified doctor and a real high-flier.

Her parents keep complaining that she is different and odd and that she has no respect for their culture. But then the UK, with all its good and bad points, is all she knows – and she is very modern and European in her attitudes.

She simply can't see why on earth she would consider having an arranged marriage, or why she should tell her parents her plans, or details of her income. She works hard and all she wants is to be true to herself and to live a 'normal' life like everyone else. But her parents feel betrayed and threatened by her lifestyle and want to have a say in her working hours, her friends, and what time she comes home each evening – and all this despite the fact that they live over a hundred miles from her.

She is extremely unhappy about the situation. She doesn't feel she can do what they want. But the rows and the almost certain estrangement from them if she fails to comply with their wishes is causing her to feel uncertain about her own values, her own judgement, her own place in life and her own future.

The sad thing is that her parents are lovely, hard-working people. And she is a really special young woman. It's just that the two generations are very different from each other.

She feels this difference keenly. Perhaps she always has – and the legacy of all this trouble is that although to outsiders she appears supremely confident and capable and happy, inside she is desperately lacking in that core of positive conviction that we all need in order to wake up each morning and be able to say: 'I'm OK.'

Being different doesn't mean that you're hateful, bad or wrong. Just different.

Children of all UDFYPs are often left with the feeling that they're:

- ungrateful;
- strangely different;
- odd;
- defective;
- unlovable.

As an adult, if you feel different from your parents, you need to find – and speak with – your own voice. It's important not to dismiss everything about your family out of hand. But neither should you allow yourself to be held back or forced into a life that you know is not right for you.

Chapter Four Key Points:

1 Events in childhood have a huge impact on the development of self-esteem.

2 It can be helpful to:
- acknowledge the kind of upbringing you had;
- accept the kind of upbringing you had;
- make allowances for your parents and their mistakes;
- challenge their views or criticisms of you.

3 You should make a decision about how much contact it's healthy for you to have with your parents.

5

Tackling Negative Inner Commentaries (NICs)

I wonder how often you say harsh and demeaning things about yourself – either to a partner, a friend, a colleague, or a boss? Maybe you don't even know you're doing it. But people with poor self-esteem are always putting themselves down. So I bet you've been known to say at least some of the following:

- I'm too fat for this dress.
- I'm getting too old to master this technology.
- Don't ask *me* to do it, I'm bound to muck it up.
- I'm really stupid when it comes to giving directions.
- I'm hopeless at getting organised.
- I look awful.

As I've already said in this book, it's crazy to criticise yourself – because every time you do, you reinforce false and unhelpful beliefs about yourself in your own head. And, I'm afraid, you encourage other people to believe these things about you too.

However, what you say out loud about yourself is only part of the problem. Rather more importantly, we have to look at what you think about yourself.

Believe me, people who don't regard themselves very highly criticise themselves inwardly all the time with thoughts like:

- I can't do that.
- No one likes me.
- I'm bound to fail.
- I'm not the sort of person who people fall in love with.

Damning thoughts like these really exacerbate poor self-esteem. It's important to learn to spot when you're thinking in this way – and to stop it.

This isn't easy – but it *is* possible.

I find it helps to think of these thoughts as a Negative Inner Commentary, or NIC for short. Think of a spoken commentary on a football game – well, that's pretty much what your NIC is like: it goes on and on, but it's all in your own head and it's very critical of just one person, and that person is *you*!

NICs are packed with critical thoughts about ourselves. And they're very damaging because, as they drone on and on in our heads, these thoughts are responsible for altering our mood so that we find ourselves feeling miserable, anxious, confused, ashamed, guilty, irritated, or jealous – or maybe a combination of these emotions.

These feelings are horrid and upsetting – and they make poor self-esteem even worse. So to make your self-esteem *better*, you need to spot when you're lapsing into a Negative Inner Commentary, and to stop it. Once you can do this, you can learn to think more positively about yourself and you can learn to replace your NIC with a PIC, or Positive Inner Commentary.

So, the aim of this chapter is to get you to recognise that:

- You do have Negative Inner Commentaries (NICs).
- You often activate them.
- NICs are responsible for lots of distressed and disturbed feelings.
- You can learn to spot your NICs and, with practice, you can learn to stop them and replace them with PICs instead.

You may have NICs cropping up all over the place. And you may feel that stopping them and altering them is too big a task to cope with. But, what you will discover, as you examine your NICs, is that they're all very similar. Or, to put it another way, the same negative thoughts about yourself crop up again and again. So, situations may be different, but the basic thoughts in your NICs won't alter very much.

After reading the last chapter (which is all about parents), you may already have identified some of the thoughts that crop up time and time again.

Thoughts like:

- I'm no good.
- I can't do things.
- I'm odd.
- I'm unattractive.
- I'm unworthy.

These recurring thoughts will form the basis of any NIC that you have – and they will frequently stem from criticisms that were levelled at you in childhood.

Unfortunately, NICs get activated at the most inconvenient times. Suppose you're in a room, waiting to be called in to an interview for a job you really, really want. And suppose that there's a woman sitting nearby – also waiting to be interviewed – who looks attractive and confident. How do you feel as you look at her?

Well, if you've got great self-esteem, you'll obviously notice her and you may even wonder if she has a better chance of getting the job than you. But you won't disturb yourself over it. So your thoughts will form a Positive Inner Commentary (PIC) and will go something like this:

'That other candidate looks bright and capable, but then, *I'm* bright and capable too. I've got a good chance of getting this job. Still, you never know exactly what employers are looking for, so although I really hope I'll get it, I won't be devastated if it goes to someone else. There are plenty of other jobs I can try for. Anyway,

I bet I'll do well in the interview – and that might clinch it for me.'

If you don't have much self-esteem however, you'll activate a Negative Inner Commentary, which will go something like this:

'People like me don't get wonderful jobs. I can't do this. I'm hopeless. My CV may look OK, but I know I'm stupid. That woman will get the job.'

So, a PIC comprises positive and realistic thoughts in any situation, but an NIC doesn't. Instead, it holds you back in life and stops you from valuing yourself properly. And it generates unhelpful feelings and moods – such as sadness, hopelessness, guilt or panic. I'm going to encourage you to learn to spot when you activate an NIC, and I'm also going to help you to learn to replace it with a PIC.

When you get good at this, you'll find that you can prevent bad moods and feelings from taking hold, and this in turn will help your good self-esteem habit, because you won't spend so much time criticising yourself and feeling miserable.

I must just warn you that NICs tend to be well ingrained – and hard to get rid of. But with each passing day you will:

- be more aware of them;
- be more alert to the fact that they happen;
- stop accepting them as the truth.

Remember: just because you believe something very strongly – such as: 'I'm hopeless' – it *doesn't* mean that it's true and that you really *are* hopeless. Not at all.

Sometimes in our quest for self-discovery, it helps to read about other people's experiences. So let me tell you about two women – Marienka and Vivienne – and about how they learned to deal with their NICs.

Marienka's story

Marienka is thirty-six. She's got a degree in psychology and is now a school teacher.

She's attractive, funny and popular. And yet she is often depressed and she gets very anxious about work and relationships.

One day, she confided in me about her previous evening's 'disastrous' date.

Her new boyfriend, Andrew, had come for supper. He seemed to be everything she'd been looking for in a man as he was kind, humorous, good-looking, considerate and very clever.

The date had begun well. They'd ordered a Chinese take-away and were chatting and watching television. It turned out that Andrew was very keen on the programme *University Challenge*, which was on that evening, so they settled down to watch it.

Andrew was quicker than the teams when it came to answering many of the questions, and Marienka was amazed by his breadth of knowledge.

Then a question came up on classical music and, much to the surprise of both of them, Marienka answered it before everyone else. Andrew gave her a playful punch on her arm: 'Clever girl. How did you know that?' he asked.

She shrugged her shoulders. 'I just did,' she smiled.

This tiny – seemingly insignificant – moment went on to ruin the evening.

As the programme continued, Marienka got more and more upset that Andrew could answer so many questions. She also grew increasingly anxious about the classical music answer that she'd got right. She felt worried because she had guessed the answer. Should she have told Andrew that her response had just been an inspired guess, she asked herself? What would happen now if he expected her to know all about classical music? How would she explain herself? What would he think of her once he realised that she hadn't a clue about classical music – or indeed about lots of other things?

Her mood plummeted – and before long, Andrew decided to go home. As he left he said:

'I don't understand what's gone wrong tonight. We were having such a great time – but then you just seemed to go into a shell where I couldn't get to you . . . I'll call you . . . sometime.'

Marienka began to cry as she finished her story.

'He won't call me,' she sobbed. 'I just go a bit odd with people. And it ruins things. But I can't help myself.'

'Perhaps you can, though,' I said.

'I can't.'

'Well, will you try – just for about five minutes?'

'I suppose so,' she said.

So I got her to cast her mind back to the previous evening and I asked her what thoughts were going through her mind before she got into her quiet, silent and miserable mood.

'Well,' she said, 'I was thinking quite happy thoughts to begin with such as: he's nice. He's clever. He's easy to get on with.'

'And how did that change?'

'I started to think other things.'

'Like what?'

'Like – he's really very, very clever.'

'And . . . ?'

'And he might not want to bother with me.'

'Why shouldn't he want to bother with you?'

'I'm not sure.'

'OK, so why don't you tell me about the actual incident when you answered the classical music question.'

'I don't know what to say about it.'

'Well, were you pleased you answered it?'

'In a way.'

'In what way *weren't* you pleased?'

'Something to do with guessing it. I didn't really know the answer. It was a cheat.'

'Do you think that guessing is the same as cheating?'

'Well . . . no . . .'

'Wouldn't you say that lots of answers in quizzes are guesses? Or that there may be things that are buried so deep in our minds we didn't realise we really knew them?'

'Maybe.'

'So was that all that was worrying you – or was there more to it?'

'I think I was really upset because I should have told him that I'd guessed the answer.'

'Why didn't you?'

'Because I wanted him to think that I really knew it.'

'And that thought upset you so much that it made you really sad – so sad that it ruined the evening?'

'Yes, I know it's pathetic, but it really did.'

'So, what was going through your mind when you felt upset that you hadn't told him you'd guessed the answer?'

'I thought: he can't be interested in me.'

'And why did you think that?'

'Because he's so clever.'

'And why would him being clever be a threat to the relationship?'

'Because I'm so stupid.'

At this point, Marienka's tears – which had almost dried up – re-started with a vengeance. She cried and cried and was obviously deeply distressed.

'Why do you say that?'

'Because I *am* stupid. I know I am. I've always known it. I spend my whole life trying to cover up so that other people don't notice it.'

'So you've always known you were stupid?'

'Yes.'

'Well, can you remember the first time you felt stupid, or a time when you felt stupid very early on in your life?'

Marienka said nothing. But as I watched her she seemed to become tinier and paler. Then she started talking about her childhood.

It turned out that Marienka had been born in Czechoslovakia. Her parents were highly educated and liberal. They were university professors, and they were quite politically active during the troubled days of 1968. Somehow, they managed to get out of the country – taking toddler Marienka with them – just in the nick of time before Russian tanks stormed into their country.

They moved through several different countries over the next couple of years before settling in England. Life was tough but gradually it improved, and both parents eventually got university posts. The family blossomed and grew. A brother and later a sister arrived: confident children, who had never known a life other than the safe and secure one in the UK.

Marienka, on the other hand, did not feel confident. In fact, she felt she was very dumb compared with the rest of the family.

'Why did you feel that?' I asked.

Suddenly, Marienka had a vision of herself at primary school.

'I couldn't understand the language,' she cried. 'I couldn't work out what was going on. Especially when it came to reading. I was slow and I couldn't understand anything. And I couldn't chat to the other children in the playground . . .'

'But you were doing everything in what was a foreign language for you,' I reminded her.

Marienka ignored me. 'And a girl who sat next to me used to say: "You're stupid." And she was right. I was stupid.'

'And how old were you?'

'I don't know. Five . . . Six . . .'

'And why should you have been able to read English – and speak it? What nationality were you?'

'Czech, of course.'

'And how many of those English children could have gone to a Czech school and spoken their language?'

'That's not the point.'

'Why isn't it the point?'

'Well, they didn't have to.'

'Just because you had to, and you found it difficult, doesn't mean you're stupid, does it?'

'I think it does.'

'OK. Let's work out how stupid you were. If 100 per cent is excessively stupid – the most stupid anyone can possibly be – and 0 per cent is incredibly bright, what rating would you give your five-year-old self?'

'About ninety."

'Ninety per cent stupid?'

'Yes.'

'And what about the Marienka of today, what rating will you give her?'

'Well, I can speak English OK, but I'm still pretty stupid. I'd say 70 per cent.'

'Well, now let's look at things from a slightly different angle. Suppose there's a little girl – aged about five – who is forced to leave her country because of political unrest. Say, somewhere like Iraq. Anyway, she comes to school in the UK. At first it feels very strange to her. The culture's completely different and she speaks very little English – and neither do her family. Do you think she's stupid because she doesn't understand everything at school and is slower to learn to read than some of the British children?'

'Well – no.'

'Why isn't she stupid?'

'Well, she's only just got here. Everything's different. There's been a lot of turmoil – and you can' t learn English in five minutes.'

'So, if you had to give her a rating between 100 per cent for utterly stupid and 0 per cent meaning she was incredibly bright, what would you give her?'

'Maybe about twenty.'

'Why was the other little girl – the one from Iraq – so different from you?'

'I don't know . . . I just have never thought about things this way.'

'I think it's time that you did! When I heard your story, I was actually thinking what a brave and bright child you must have been. How else could you have come from Czechoslovakia, undergone all sorts of upheaval and then gone straight into mainstream schooling here? That was fantastic. In fact I genuinely feel lost in admiration of you.'

'Do you?'

'I really do. So shall we think again about your five-year-old self? Is it possible you've been a bit hard on her?'

'Perhaps.'

'I find it rather painful that she's got nothing but criticism and vilification from you – when actually she deserves lots of praise and love because she was brave and determined,' I said. 'How do you feel about her now?'

At this point, Marienka began to weep again – silent, heartfelt tears. And I could see that she was re-thinking her past and getting in touch with that five-year-old's difficulties and sorrow – and beginning to see that, as her five-year-old self, she had actually behaved well and bravely.

Funnily enough, people almost always cry when they come into contact with their own good points, and this usually helps them. It's as if the warmth of their goodness finally melts a great big emotional iceberg that they've been trapped in.

Marienka was very quiet for several minutes.

'So,' I said eventually, 'what kind of rating for stupidity would you like to give the five-year-old Marienka now?'

'Quite a low one – I mean, she wasn't actually stupid, was she? Just bewildered – and not British. I'll give her 10 per cent. I can't give her 0 per cent because she wasn't good at sums – and I'm still not!'

Marienka giggled. She was looking much happier.

'That's quite a difference then, isn't it?' I asked. 'Only 10 per cent stupid when she was 90 per cent stupid five minutes ago. She *has* improved!'

Marienka laughed again.

'OK. Shall we now look again at the rating for the grown-up Marienka? Before you give it, I'd like you to think about everything you've overcome, and also to remember that you went on to get a degree, and that you now hold down a job in quite a tough school where your pupils like you, and work hard for you. When you consider all these things, what do you think your stupidity rating is today? As before, 100 per cent is just about as stupid as you can get.'

'About 10 per cent.'

'And is it still only 10 per cent when you guess a question in *University Challenge*?'

'Oh – I don't know.' Marienka looked worried again.

'OK, how many times do the contestants make correct guesses in an average edition of the programme, do you think?'

'Dunno. Quite a few. Maybe twenty or so.'

'Yes – at least that, I imagine.'

'Are the contestants stupid when they make those guesses?'

'No – they just don't actually know that particular answer. Maybe it's nothing to do with the subjects they're studying, for example.'

'No. And of course what did you study at university?'

'Psychology.'

'And when you were watching the programme, what was the subject of the question where you guessed the right answer?'

'Classical music.'

'And have you ever studied classical music?'

'No. And it's not even one of my interests.'

'So how stupid was it that you guessed that question?'

'OK, it wasn't stupid.'

'But was it stupid that you didn't tell Andrew it was a guess?'

'Perhaps a tiny bit. But then I haven't known him for long. So maybe I should keep some secrets. Anyway, maybe some of his right answers were guesses.'

'So what was the worst thing about the evening, do you think?'

'It was the mood I got myself into.'

'And can you see how you got into that mood?'

'Yes – I got into it because of the thoughts going through my mind.'

'Is it possible that thoughts about incompetence are responsible for a lot of your unhappy moods?'

Marienka thought for a moment. 'Yes – I get huffy at school if I suspect someone isn't taking me seriously. I feel cross with my parents when they talk about my brother's or sister's achievements, because I decide they're saying that I must be unintelligent in comparison. My last boyfriend used to laugh at me because I didn't know where places like Bosnia were when they came on the news. He made me feel really depressed . . .'

'But did *he* make you depressed? Or did your depression happen because you had a Negative Inner Commentary at work, telling you that you're stupid?'

'I suppose it was because of the Negative Inner Commentary.'

Marienka had uncovered something very important. She had discovered for herself that situations in themselves don't upset us; it's our NICs that actually cause us grief. Or as the Stoic philosopher, Epictetus, said: 'It's not things that upset us, it's our *view* of things.'

Most of us have Negative Inner Commentaries. They are unique to us. But Marienka's went something like this:

- I can't do this.
- I don't deserve this relationship.
- Andrew's too clever for me.
- I'm going to be found out.
- I'm stupid.

Two of those phrases in Marienka's NIC that day were phrases that she tended to think every time she got upset – whether the situation was to do with a boyfriend, other friends, her parents or her job. They were:

- I can't do this.
- I'm stupid.

Now, you may never have had the trauma that Marienka had as a child. But I'm sure that you have NICs operating in all sorts of difficult situations and I'm equally sure that, like Marienka, some of the phrases in your commentaries recur time and time and time again.

Just mull over what happened to Marienka – and have a think about whether her story can help you with your own problems.

Meanwhile, let me tell you about Vivienne.

Vivienne's story

Vivienne is a journalist. She's in her mid-forties and is very successful and respected.

The world of journalism is not only highly competitive, it's also very uncertain. And, from time to time, Vivienne finds herself out of a job – usually when there's an editorial re-shuffle, or a management-drive to save money.

No journalist likes being sacked – but most of them recognise that these days it happens to everyone, so they just accept the unpredictability of their existence.

Unfortunately, Vivienne can't bear all this insecurity, so she feels anxious most of the time.

If her Editor goes off on maternity leave, Vivienne becomes convinced that the Acting Editor will seize the opportunity to sack her.

If a newspaper that she works for is sold to a new owner, she worries herself sick about the redundancies that will almost certainly follow.

On such occasions, she frequently gets so tense that she develops a thumping migraine and has to go home.

At the time of our story, Vivienne had a great job as the Features Editor on a quality Sunday newspaper.

One day, she was talking to the Editor's secretary – the source of all office gossip – who let slip that the Editor had been in meetings with the management all day.

'Probably big changes on the way,' said the secretary, with more than a hint of relish.

Immediately, Vivienne felt so shaky and tearful that she made an excuse to return to her own desk. She tried to calm herself, but those words 'big changes' kept haunting her. If there were to be 'big changes' this must mean cutbacks in staff. And Vivienne knew – just knew – that this would mean *her* job would go.

Her heart was racing, she felt sick, and her mind flooded with doom-laden thoughts:

- I can't stand it if I lose this job.
- I'll never get another job as good as this one.
- I may never work again.
- Everything's going to be hateful.
- I'll never recover from this.

Now, the interesting fact is that Vivienne had been through several changes in employment and she would doubtless cope with another. Also, there was no evidence that the Editor's meetings were anything to do with jobs – Vivienne's, or anyone else's. Even if she were sacked, how could she possibly *know* that she'd never get another job, that everything would be hateful and that she'd never recover?

Well, of course she couldn't know these things. You and I can see that. But, at the time, Vivienne couldn't. This is a very good example of how an individual can disturb herself – and how quickly she can spiral down into a despairing state.

But why does someone disturb themselves so quickly and so distressingly?

It's because they've activated a Negative Inner Commentary.

Vivienne's Negative Inner Commentary was sounding in her head, telling her that she was bound to lose her job, and so she spent the rest of the day feeling deeply anxious.

At last she got home. But when she arrived, she found a note – a loving note – from her partner saying that he was going to be away that night as his mother, who lived fifty miles away, was ill and he'd gone to see her in hospital. The note also said that he would count the hours till he could be back with her and that he loved her with all his heart.

Vivienne felt even more rejected. In her distress, she didn't even notice the loving message in the note. She just felt alone and miserable. In fact it felt like the whole world was against her. So she opened a bottle of wine, and proceeded to get on the outside of it rather too quickly. This helped initially, but as the evening wore on, and she opened another bottle – and never quite got round to eating anything – she felt more and more depressed, till she was practically suicidal.

The next morning, which fortunately was a Saturday, she sat sipping coffee and nursing a headache. She suddenly decided that she had to stop behaving like a 'flakey drama queen' and get herself together.

Vivienne actually had quite a lot of insight into how her mind worked. But she knew that she'd never been able to handle what she saw as rejections at work, and also that she always reacted badly to any hint of rejection by a partner. The previous night's note from her partner had not been a rejection. But it had felt like it – especially on top of her anxieties about her job.

'What the hell's wrong with me?' she asked herself.

Sitting there, she tried to piece together what had happened at work. She reminded herself how often she had lost jobs in the past – and indeed how often all her colleagues had lost jobs too. Sometimes she'd been out of work for a while, but she'd always found something else. Frequently something better.

'So why do I mind so much?'

She poured herself more coffee and tussled with her thoughts.

She got a piece of paper and wrote on it: 'Why do I mind so much if I lose a job?' Then she looked at it for ages.

After a while, she wrote down some positive points – such as the fact that she'd get a decent pay-off if she was sacked, and that she was good at getting new jobs. Looking at the paper she felt slightly more cheerful, but she knew she hadn't got to the bottom of what was distressing her.

Suddenly a different thought occurred to her. I mind, she thought, because I'm frightened they don't want me.

She realised immediately that this thought was very important because it really resonated with her and made her want to cry.

'They don't want me,' she said aloud. And then she said it over and over again. It was an agonising thought. People *must* want her: it felt like the end of the world if they didn't; she couldn't stand it.

Then other things came into her mind. She found herself thinking about her mother: a mother she found it almost impossible to please.

Had her mother ever really wanted her? She could recall being told she had been a 'mistake'. And she could also remember her mother describing Vivienne's birth in disturbingly graphic detail. She had first heard the story when she was twelve, but had been treated to re-runs of it on numerous occasions.

'I was in labour for hours,' her mother had told her. 'You took so long to come. It was agony. Agony. I couldn't bear it and I was trying to knock myself unconscious by banging my head on the wall – anything, anything to stop the excruciating pain.'

The memory of her mother's bitter expression and vehement speech was intensely painful for Vivienne, and she felt miserable, sad, confused and unloved as she recalled it. But, in the midst of these overwhelming feelings, Vivienne began to see that something about her birth – and her mother's attitude to her – was relevant to her anxieties about work.

In fact, she realised that everything that disturbed her was to do with being wanted, whether it was to do with employers, or her boyfriend or her other friends.

Feeling unwanted was a terrifying feeling. Her mother had not wanted her. Not much, anyway.

Her father had loved her and her grandparents had doted on her. But she could recall how bleak she had often felt as a child. Bleak, alone – and unwanted.

Unwanted. That was the key.

Maybe my mother wanted me in her own way, she thought. But it just wasn't enough. And I didn't feel as if she did. But my dad and grandparents wanted me. And I am wanted by my partner and my friends. And I am wanted at work – but even if I'm not, they're not rejecting *me*. Not Vivienne. They may choose to dispense with my work because they've got to make financial cuts, but they're not getting rid of me because they don't *want* me.

That Saturday morning Vivienne re-thought her whole life. And she did it without any therapy, but just by using her own common-sense.

I only know about it because she confided in me when she heard I was writing this book.

Vivienne managed to identify that she had a NIC that berated herself for not being important enough, not special enough – and not wanted.

Identifying her NIC was not the end of the story. Obviously, a lifetime of thinking that she was unwanted was not going to disappear overnight. But Vivienne worked hard on spotting the moment when she activated NICs – which were almost always to do with fears that she wasn't wanted – and she started to ask herself whether her thoughts about being unwanted in any given situation were actually *true*.

She realised something else that was very important.

'I think,' she told me, 'that my mother's attitude to me as a child, has always affected how I think and feel and act now. If, for example, my partner's a bit cross about something, I see my mother's angry eyes staring out at me. And if some boss or other criticises my work, I feel about six years old – and as if my mother's telling me off.

'But what I've come to see is that none of these people *is* my mother. So I really don't have to put myself through this torture. And that's very liberating.'

Vivienne soon got into the habit of spotting when she activated a NIC. And she learned to stop her thoughts and then ask herself whether or not they were actually true. When she conceded that they weren't, she replaced her NIC with some thoughts that were more positive and realistic: a PIC.

'I am unwanted' is a very painful, but quite common NIC. Is it yours? If so, maybe you can get some idea of how to deal with it through identifying with Vivienne's story.

Common situations that activate our NICs

Let us now look at some situations where we're likely to activate our NICs.

Someone, like Marienka, whose NICs are always about being stupid, will be very distressed in situations like these:

- if she forgets someone's name, or forgets an appointment;
- if she fails an exam;
- if she can't understand a television programme;
- if she doesn't get a joke;
- if someone criticises her work;
- if she's on a course and finds the course-work difficult;
- if she misses a train.

And someone like Vivienne, whose Negative Inner Commentaries are about how unlovable and how unwanted they are, will activate NICs in situations like these:

- if her boyfriend has to go away on business;
- if her boyfriend, her boss, colleagues, or other friends are angry with her;
- if her relationship ends;
- if she smiles at her boss, and the boss doesn't smile back;
- if she sends a present to a friend and the friend forgets to write or phone to thank her;
- if a sibling or friend doesn't phone when she said she would.

So if, for example, someone like Marienka doesn't understand her work when she's on a course, she'll immediately brand herself as stupid and feel horribly miserable – even though the truth is that everyone on the course is having difficulties and the lecturer is hopeless at explaining the subject.

And if someone like Vivienne smiles at her boss one morning and the boss doesn't smile back, her NIC will tell her that she's disliked or unwanted, and she'll quickly plunge into gloom – when the simple truth may be that her boss hasn't put her contact lenses in!

What situations really get *you* going? Are you someone who gets upset easily about your personal lovability? Or are you more likely to become anxious or saddened by a situation that sparks off thoughts and feelings about your performance?

From today, give yourself a little task to do. Every time you're upset by a situation, write down what happened. If you keep doing this, you'll begin to see a pattern emerging and before long you'll be able to spot what your NIC is saying in these situations – and why you get upset.

Identifying your NICs

We now know quite a lot about the sort of situations which are likely to activate NICs – but we also know that it isn't the situations themselves that cause the trouble, it's the NICs, or, in other words, it's what we're thinking.

We've seen how Marienka and Vivienne spotted their NICs and then learned to deal with them. And you are now – I hope – beginning to make a note of situations that cause you upset.

So, where do we go from here?

We need to look at a situation that has upset you recently, and to work out what your own, personal NIC was telling you.

Ask yourself:

1. What was the situation?
2. What was your mood?
3. And what was going through your mind to generate that mood?

It will help to write down the answers to these three questions. Next, take a look at what you've written as the answer to the third question: what was going through your mind to generate that mood? You'll find that what you've written is actually the Negative Inner Commentary that you activated in that situation.

For example, you may have got very upset about not getting a promotion that you wanted. And you may have worked out that the thoughts causing your distress were:

'No one values or respects me. I do try hard, but it gets me nowhere. The whole thing's pointless. I'm not as good at things as other people. I'm hopeless.'

The next step is to look at another upsetting scenario. Perhaps this time the situation is about you and your childminder. Maybe you're late home from work and the childminder is cross with you. You feel very upset about this and you work out that your NIC has gone something like this:

'I can't seem to schedule my day properly. Other people manage things much better than me. I don't know why I even bother to try to get things right, because they always go wrong. I'm hopeless.'

As you can see, these are different situations, but the NICs have a lot in common, and many of the thoughts forming the NICs are identical.

Keep looking at upsetting situations like these and you will find that a definite pattern will emerge. And, like Marienka and Vivienne, you'll probably find that though situations alter, you tend to activate similar NICs all the time and that some of the thoughts in these NICs occur over and over and over again.

To help you establish *exactly* what you're thinking, here's a list of the thoughts that most commonly run through NICs:

- I'm stupid.
- I'm unwanted.
- I'm unloved, or unlovable.
- I'm boring.
- I'm in the way.
- I'm annoying.
- I'm unattractive.
- I'm different.
- I can't do it.
- I'm lazy.
- I'm bound to get things wrong.
- I'm not respected.
- I'm feeble.
- I'm hopeless.

I know that what I'm asking you to do is not easy – and also that it's time consuming. But all I can say is that this chapter in the book is the most vital one if you are to get the habit of good self-esteem, because acquiring good self-esteem depends upon healthy and positive thinking. If you can persist with sorting out which situations upset you, and identifying what your NIC is saying to you, then you will be well on the way to discovering why you've thought so badly about yourself up until now.

Changing your NIC into a PIC

By now, I hope you can accept that we all have NICs. And that NICs crop up all the time to disturb us.

I hope, too, that you've made a start on working out what your own NICs are saying to you.

Already you're more aware of how you think and of how that is damaging you. But to effect *real* change, you need to challenge the truth of your NICs and then to change them into Positive Inner Commentaries.

To do this, you have to become your own Truth Detective, so that you can establish whether your NIC is true, or a lie. And you need to be really scrupulous about this – and persistent. Imagine you're Inspector Morse, or Hercule Poirot, digging away to get the facts of what really happened in order to solve a crime. After all, in a way, you've been committing a crime against yourself – probably for years – so you need to apply their rigorous methods to get at the truth.

Let's look again at one of the situations that has upset you recently. You've already established what your mood was. And you've probably worked out what your Negative Inner Commentary was on that occasion.

Now it's time to ask yourself a number of questions about that NIC:

- Is there any real truth in these negative thoughts?
- If I had a friend in this situation and she had these thoughts, would I think that her thoughts were justified?
- Am I telling myself that I'm hopeless, or unlovable, or unwanted simply because of one flaw, one mistake or event?
- Am I blaming myself for something which is not my fault?
- Am I taking something personally which has little to do with me?
- Am I focusing so much on my weaknesses that I don't even notice my good points?
- Am I expecting myself to be perfect?

- Am I condemning myself for things that I'd forgive in other people?
- Am I exaggerating the importance of situations that trouble me?

Find the origin of your NIC

At this point, it may also help you to establish how your NIC started – and when.

Marienka was able to discover that hers began at the age of five, when she moved to this country and had to go to school.

The origins of Vivienne's NIC were a bit more vague, but stemmed from the idea that she had been a mistake and that her mother hadn't really wanted her.

Both women were able to see that though there was *some* truth in the original NIC, the NIC was not *wholly* true.

From that understanding, they were able to change the way they had perceived the original NIC – and then to change any current NIC into a PIC.

In Marienka's case, she realised that although she had been unable to speak English, and hadn't been able to understand what was going on at school, this did *not* mean she was stupid. With the recognition that she wasn't stupid, she was then able to alter any NIC that she activated. She was able to say: 'I know I tend to think that I'm stupid, but I've got masses of evidence – both in my childhood and my adult life – to prove that I'm not, so I don't have to think these critical thoughts about myself. I am, in fact, a very bright woman.'

Vivienne was able to see that although her mother had had a bad confinement and had not been overjoyed to be a parent, this did not mean that the child Vivienne was horrible or unwantable. And just because her mum couldn't show much love, it didn't mean that Vivienne was an unlovable or unwantable little girl, it just meant that her mother was flawed and had problems of her own. Furthermore, she was able to accept that other relatives had loved her and that plenty of people in her adult life loved and wanted her.

So when situations arose that triggered off Vivienne's NIC about being unwanted, she was able to replace it with a PIC that went: 'I always think that I am unwanted. But this isn't the case. Loads of people love and want me. It looks as though I may lose this job, but I'm not the only one. And it's just about money, not about me. I'll get another job because I'm good at what I do and people want to employ me.'

You too can do exactly what Marienka and Vivienne did. You can probably work out – from looking back into your early life – how your NICs started. Then you can challenge whether the thoughts that came up at that time were true.

You'll almost certainly find that they were based in some sort of fact, but that most of your perception was wrong.

You can change that perception and then you can change how you think in today's situations. In fact, in time you'll realise that you're really bored with the old way of thinking. And you'll be able to stop your old NIC in its tracks by thinking:

'Oh, here we go again. Same old critical thoughts. Bit like a sound tape on a perpetual loop. I'm so bored with it. Thank goodness I'm learning to be more positive, so I won't have to put up with all these boring negative thoughts that are dragging me down.'

Believe me, boredom is a great way to take the importance out of NICs and to cut them down to size.

Of course your poor self-esteem habit has been reinforced by your NICs for a long time. So be patient with yourself. You won't erase them and learn to be positive at all times overnight, but every time you stop yourself from thinking and believing in the old way, give yourself a massive mental pat on the back.

Eventually, you will be able to activate PICs much more often and you'll gradually stop activating the NICs. When this happens, your self-esteem habit will blossom.

Chapter Five Key Points:

1 Recognise that you have a Negative Inner Commentary that disturbs and upsets you.
2 Keep a note of situations that particularly upset you so that you can recognise them more easily – and deal with them.
3 Try to work out from these situations what your Negative Inner Commentary is saying.
4 Look back at your life to see where your Negative Inner Commentary started.
5 Challenge the truth of the distressing thoughts and feelings which you had as a child.
6 Acknowledge that those thoughts and feelings evolved into your Negative Inner Commentary which has disturbed you ever since.
7 Challenge the truth of your Negative Inner Commentary when you're in situations that trigger it off in your adult life.
8 Work at replacing any Negative Inner Commentary with a Positive Inner Commentary.

6

Getting in Touch with Your Own Goodness

Human beings have the most amazing capacity for kindness, love, decency and goodness.

But, as I've already said, when people have poor self-esteem, they find it difficult to appreciate these very important qualities within themselves.

I've also already mentioned (in Chapter Five) that when individuals *do* start to acknowledge and enjoy their own goodness, they frequently become very tearful initially. But then their belief in themselves and their estimation of themselves begins to dramatically improve.

This chapter is all about how you can uncover your own goodness and learn to 'own' it – because when you do, you'll definitely improve your self-esteem habit.

Let me begin by telling you all about Adam:

Adam is an actor. He's shy. He's gay. And he is a delightful and good man. The trouble is that he couldn't see for himself that he was a delightful and thoroughly good man – not, that is, until he got in touch with his own goodness.

Interestingly, although Adam is a shy person, he is an excellent actor who works a lot. And not many actors can say that! He also has confidence in what he *does*. Unfortunately for him, he has always lacked confidence in who he *is*. In fact, he's very critical of himself. And his Negative Inner Commentary tends to go:

- I'm hopeless at relationships.
- I'm not attractive.
- I'm unlovable.
- I'm a disappointment to people.

You can't get much more 'down' on yourself than that, can you?

One day, I asked Adam to tell me all about his childhood. Like many sufferers of low self-esteem, Adam had been brought up in a family that looked fine from the outside, but which was actually pretty hopeless behind closed doors.

His parents were very definitely TUPs (Timid, Undemonstrative Parents) and didn't seem to understand the young Adam, who was very clever, as well as being hugely artistic.

'They were very suspicious of my theatrical nature,' he told me. 'Deep down they probably feared I was a bit of a "pansy" – which is the kind of word they'd have used. But of course they never, ever could have brought themselves to discuss my sexual orientation either to each other or to me. In fact, we still don't discuss it, and they still don't acknowledge that I'm gay – though heaven knows, all the signs are there.'

'What about grandparents?' I asked him.

'They were part of the problem. My paternal grandfather really seemed to detest me. I know he thought I was odd, and he seemed to take no interest in my academic ability despite the fact that I won a scholarship to a public school, which no one in the family had ever done before. Grandpa had had to leave school at twelve, so maybe he felt hard done by about that, which is understandable. But his big thing was sport. He loved cricket and football and he expected me – as the first grandson – to be good at both. Unfortunately, I wasn't. I was hopeless at all sports, and not interested in any of them, either. So I was obviously a big disappointment to him. He used to give me inappropriate presents – like a cricket bat, or a racing bike that was too big for me. I really dreaded Christmas and birthdays because his gifts were always unsuitable, but very generous, so I was supposed to be pleased. And he used to ring up to see if I'd oiled the bloody bat or passed my cycling proficiency test. It was a nightmare.'

'Did he live to see you achieve success in the theatre?' I asked him.

'No – but even if he had, he wouldn't have been interested. I don't think he ever set foot in a theatre in his life.'

Throughout this conversation, Adam looked uncomfortable, but he kept his emotions very much under control.

'Do you blame yourself for the difficulties at home?' I ventured.

'Don't know about that, exactly – but I was obviously different, and disappointing. I definitely didn't feel very approved of.'

'Who loved you in that family?'

'Well, probably my parents did in their own way. I think some of my aunts did . . .'

'None of this sounds very real or very affirming. You've talked about a grandfather. What about grandmothers? Were they keener on you? Did you feel that *they* were on your side?'

Adam's voice dropped almost to a whisper.

'I really adored my grandmothers,' he said. 'But I don't think either of them quite knew what to make of me. D'you know – I went back to my parents' home recently, and, in my old room, I found a collection I'd kept of letters that my grandmothers had written to the family – people wrote much more in those days. Anyway, I'd collected all these letters from the two grannies. I'd also managed to save a lock of hair from each of them . . . must have taken it from hairbrushes when I visited, I suppose. I think, on reflection, that I was a really loving little boy . . . but they seemed afraid of that love . . .'

Adam, who had remained entirely dry-eyed when talking about his so-called failings as a sportsman, now began to cry like a baby.

I watched as he felt the pain of his younger self all over again and re-experienced the agony of having a lot of love to give – but no one to give it to.

'This love you had – especially for your grandmothers – does sound very sweet, very selfless, very kind . . . very lovely . . .'

Adam sobbed even louder.

Now, this particular conversation didn't solve all of Adam's problems. But it was the start of an improvement. As I've said before, when people suddenly experience a wave of appreciation of their own goodness, they generally cry – and their tears start to melt the cold image that they've constructed round themselves. This image – which is usually that they're odd, unlovable, unattractive and don't have much to offer people – has grown up to protect them, but it's also removed them from their own real goodness and the goodness of others.

Another example of people crying when there's a focus on their goodness or good points comes from my friend Trish McDermott, who has the lovely title of Vice President of Romance at the popular and successful online dating company, Match.com.

She tells me: 'When I interact with single people at Match.com dating classes, I will occasionally meet someone who has been carrying around a good deal of emotional pain and who has seemingly forgotten how lovely and special they are. These people commonly present a rather formidable front, which is actually emotional armour that they've retreated behind. As I get to know them, it becomes very clear that they're talented, funny, fun-loving, kind and uniquely lovable. In other words, they have a lot to offer. When I point this out – really just try to remind them of something they already know deep inside – a moment of reckoning occurs which often brings tears to their eyes. I can actually see the emotional armour slip away, and a more hopeful and open person emerge. Frankly, I'm puzzled why such wonderful people can't see much of their own beauty and worth when it's so evident to me.'

What Trish says is very, very important – and it almost certainly has a message for you.

You have uniquely lovable qualities yourself, but you may have forgotten them, or buried them when hurtful things happened to you. Try to allow yourself to feel that lovableness, and that goodness. It's a bit worrying at first, but it will put you back in touch with your genuine self – and your self-esteem will improve as a result.

Now, let me tell you about Liz. She was brave, popular and intelligent. She had come to Britain from South Africa and had embarked on a whole new career in Hospital Management, which had meant her having to take several big exams while working to support herself by working nights in a Call Centre. Often, as you can probably imagine, she felt exhausted.

She was having troubles with her relationship – and the main reason for that was that she didn't value herself very much, so she found it hard to accept that anyone might want her. (Her feelings may well strike a chord with you.)

We got on to *why* she didn't believe in herself – and it became clear it was something to do with her mother, with whom she had a rather difficult relationship. In fact it was *because* the relationship was so difficult, that she had come to England in the first place – to escape her parent!

'I never felt special to my mother,' she told me.

'Give me an example,' I said.

Liz thought for a while, then she told me about one occasion just before her mother's birthday.

'I asked Mum what she would like as a present,' she said.

'How old were you at the time?' I asked.

'Maybe . . . ten . . .'

'And what happened?'

'She answered me in a very cross kind of voice. She said: "I don't really mind – so long as you don't give me anything like that horrible bottle of perfume someone gave me last year. It was awful. How could *anyone* have bought me that?" '

Liz looked very distressed at this memory, so I asked her what happened next.

'Well,' she said. 'I asked my mother which bottle of perfume she meant and she told me to go and look on the top of the bathroom cabinet. I climbed up to see – and found the bottle *I'd* bought her the year before. It had hardly been touched. But I had saved up all my money for it – and I had bought it for her with such love. I was always trying to please her . . . I felt really horrible that day. Horrid. Stupid. Crass . . .'

'You must have been a very loving little girl to have saved up your money and bought your mum a bottle of perfume?' I suggested.

Liz began to cry. 'It was pointless, though. She hated it. I don't think I've *ever* managed to give my mother a present she liked.'

'And is that your fault?'

Liz blew her nose and had a think. 'I was trying my best. I was trying to love her. I was loving and . . . considerate. It wouldn't have killed her to have splashed on the perfume and pretended she loved it. That's what I would do if my daughter bought me perfume.'

'So was it your fault?' I asked again.

'D'you know,' Liz said, very slowly. 'I don't think it was. She was just difficult to please. She's still difficult to please, come to that.'

'But as a child you were giving her real, authentic love. And you were trying hard.'

Liz began to sob. 'I was. I was. I *was* quite a sweet little girl – and loving too.'

'Yes, I'm sure you were. And you're a very decent, kind and nice woman. A woman who deserves love. A woman who has love to give and is lovable in return.'

Liz's mother's actions had been largely responsible for starting up Liz's Negative Inner Commentary. But by looking back and by being honest – and by allowing herself to get in touch with her own goodness – Liz began to see that she had gained a false perception of herself as a child which had stayed with her as an adult. And from that day, step by step, her relationship improved – because she valued herself more. And this led to her cultivating a habit of much more positive self-esteem.

Of course, you don't always have to go back to your childhood to get in touch with your own goodness. Often people are doing kind and generous things all the time – but they simply don't count them because they're too busy being hard on themselves.

I'd like to repeat an anecdote that I first told in my earlier book in this series: *Get the Happiness Habit.* I apologise if you have read this before, but so many readers have told me that this particular illustration was a big help to them, that I've decided to use it again.

Carol came to me when she was depressed after being made redundant. She believed that the redundancy proved she was ineffective and not very clever – and also that it was all her fault. But there was no evidence for her belief. Her company had shed jobs worldwide and she was just one of a large number of casualties in their cutbacks.

Anyway, we worked together for two or three weeks: she turned up on time and did the homework I set her, but she kept me at arm's length. And although she was obviously very sad, she never cried.

One day she was going on about how hopeless and how stupid she was and how she must be a very weak person to be so sad. I listened to her self-criticism for a while. Then I asked her to tell me what her good points were.

She looked at me as if I was mad, and as if I hadn't been listening to her tirade against herself.

When I pressed her, she told me she couldn't think of anything. But eventually, after much persistence on my part, she told me how every year she used to take all the junior members of staff out for a Christmas lunch. Carol was not the head of that department, but her boss was a very stingy guy who never showed that he valued anyone else in the office.

'I thought it was awful that my boss didn't thank the staff. Many of them were quite poorly paid, but they were mostly keen and worked very hard. He didn't even send them Christmas cards. So I started taking them all out – once a year.'

'And were they pleased?' I asked.

'Well, they were, actually. We always had a very lively and happy lunch, and they did seem grateful. In fact, they clubbed together every year and bought me a little present to thank me.'

Carol began to cry as she told her story.

'They must have liked and valued you very much, then. And they must have been very grateful that you took it upon yourself to show that *someone* appreciated their work,' I suggested.

She didn't answer because by now she was convulsed with sobs.

That was a definitive moment for Carol. Her harsh self-critical and miserable veneer was melted by her own goodness and it put her in touch with a kinder, softer more vulnerable and more human side of herself.

There is kindness and decency in us all. And, for us to enjoy a habit of good self-esteem, we need to recognise this goodness and kindness and decency in ourselves.

So – how are you going to get in touch with your goodness?

Write down examples of your goodness as a child

In this chapter, you've read some examples of kindness and goodness in children that was not recognised or reciprocated. Did this happen to you? Sit quietly and think about this. What can you remember?

If you can remember incidents – just as Adam and Liz did – write them down. Look at what you've written. Try to think yourself into the skin of your younger self.

- How did you feel?
- How did your parents or an older person react?
- Did they respond to your love and kindness?
- If not – what could their reasons have been?
- How would *you* react as an adult if a child expressed love or kindness to you?

Re-visit your younger self

As well as challenging the reasons for your feelings about your own goodness, you can go one step further. You can re-visit your younger self.

To do this, you need to set aside some time when you can be very quiet and entirely alone.

You should sit, or lie, and then allow yourself to breathe very deeply and evenly, and to relax. Continue your deep breathing for at least five minutes before you do anything else.

Next, pick some way of transporting yourself back in time – in other words, you can design your own mental Time Machine. You can imagine Dr Who's tardis if you like. Or you can imagine yourself floating back through time on a cloud.

My own preferred method – which you can certainly borrow if you wish – is to imagine that I'm in a lift. Once inside, I find an extra, magic button: a secret button that no one knows about. I press that button and the lift goes down and down and down – gathering speed and taking me back in time to my childhood. I choose when to stop the lift, and when I leave it – as the adult I am now – I discover a younger version of me, waiting to communicate with me. I imagine a conversation with her. She tells me about various incidents in her life and I sympathise with her. I give her a big hug. And I tell her that I can feel her goodness and kindness, and that she will be all right, and that her life will become happier.

When I'm ready, I hug her again and say goodbye, but I tell her that I'll come and see her again. Then I get back in my lift and leave.

This is a technique that you can try on your own. But you might also like to do it under hypnosis with a qualified therapist. Full details about finding such a practitioner are available in the Help Yourself Guide at the end of the book.

Re-visiting your younger self is a very healing experience and it helps many people.

The goodness record

Now that you perhaps know more about your goodness as a child, I'd like you to become much more aware of your goodness as an adult.

One way you can do this is to keep a daily 'goodness record'. It's possible that to tackle this you'll need to overcome a kind of resistance that I've mentioned elsewhere in the book: a resistance that stops you from 'blowing your own trumpet'. You may well have been told as a child to put yourself last. Not to boast, or show off – and these commands may have left you with a lifelong belief that you shouldn't praise yourself, or expect praise. This habit, which has been generated by early conditioning, is one you need to break if you are to get a *new* habit of positive self-esteem.

Just remember: you *are* allowed to praise yourself and it is *healthy* to appreciate your good points, In fact, if you don't, you'll be very lucky if anyone else does.

The daily record will help you to be aware of the goodness that you generate.

You can use a diary for this – if you've got a spare one that you don't use for any other purpose – but any old notebook will do. All you do is write down the date each day, and then record three occasions when you have been kind, or honourable, or loving. It may be that you've bought a copy of *The Big Issue*. Or that you rang up a friend because she's having a bad time. Or it could just be that you smiled warmly at someone who was looking very fed up on your crowded train that morning.

Get into the habit of doing this every single day of your life.

I also want you to record goodness and kindness shown to you by *other* people. After you've recorded your own goodness, write down three events – every day – that demonstrate someone else's kindness and goodness to *you*.

How does this help, you may ask? Well, as I've said before, as we learn to love and value ourselves more, we tend to notice kindness and goodness in others.

When we don't care much for ourselves, we often write off other people too. We say: 'She's a complete bitch.' Or: 'He's just an uneducated lout.' And these feelings don't help us. In fact, they are very miserable feelings which leave us with a sense that everything and everybody is pretty hopeless and horrible.

But when we are in touch with our own goodness – and also in touch with the goodness of others – we feel as if we're a more significant player in the world as we want it to be, and we activate a sense of bonding with other people. We also begin to notice that the woman we dismissed as 'a bitch' is working herself into the ground to pay for her talented child to have piano lessons from a highly regarded, but expensive, teacher. Or that the 'uneducated lout' runs a football team for kids in a very deprived area.

It's very easy to feel isolated when you have poor self-esteem and to lock everyone else out of your life. But once you get into the habit of looking for goodness in yourself and in others, you'll begin to relate to others in a much more positive way. This will increase your feelings of happiness and self-worth.

So, make a note in your notebook if someone smiles at you. Or when your partner gives you a hug before leaving for work. Or when a colleague at work offers to bring you a cup of tea from the machine.

Soon you'll find that you're noticing goodness – either done by you or to you – all the time and in the most unlikely places. In addition, you'll become aware of goodness that has nothing to do with you. For example, you might see a young shop assistant being extra kind and patient and helpful to an elderly woman who is confused about money. And when you notice this, it will give you a warm feeling: a feeling that acknowledges that there's lots of goodness about – and that life is sweet.

Being in touch with goodness – our own and other people's – feeds our souls. And this increases our feelings that:

- we are valuable to ourselves and other people;
- life is worth living;
- we have rights;
- we are deserving of love.

It also helps us to acknowledge that everyone else is valuable – and that they have rights too.

The Speedy (ten-minute) Soother

This is a technique which I described in *Get the Happiness Habit* and which I've also mentioned earlier in this book. It's important because, in my view, no one can fully develop their good self-esteem habit unless they can be quiet and comfortable when they're alone in their own space.

So, you need to plan to do this when you're on your own and not likely to be disturbed. It's only for ten minutes daily – and everyone can find the time if they really try. You can sit or lie down, then all you have to do is to breathe. Nothing else. You don't read, listen to music, or think about the shopping you've got to get later. You just exist, quietly, peacefully and contentedly. This is your time to just 'be'. You're entitled to it. And if you allow yourself to do this daily, you will find that it provides you with an oasis of calm and a sense of being 'OK' in your own skin.

You deserve this 'soul' time. You deserve to enjoy it. And you definitely deserve the improvement in your self-esteem that you'll get as a result of it.

Chapter Six Key Points:

1 Look back into your childhood and find examples of your own kind and loving qualities.
2 Keep a diary of three kind and honourable things that you do every day, and also of three equally decent things that other people do for or to you.
3 Do the Speedy (ten-minute) Soother.

7

How to Be the Sort of Person That Other People Like

Up till now, this book has been all about changing how you *think*. These changes – as I'm sure you know by now – are absolutely crucial if you are to get a good self-esteem habit. So it's vital that you continue to:

- examine your thoughts;
- be aware that thoughts create moods;
- identify your Negative Inner Commentaries (NICs) – and change them into Positive Inner Commentaries (PICs);
- get in touch with your own goodness – and that of others.

But while you're doing all this, over the next few chapters, I'm going to help you to develop more skills in various situations. And to do so, I'll be giving you some practical hints and tips that will make your life easier.

These won't be fantastically effective if you try to do them *instead* of changing how your mind operates. But if you use them in *addition* to the work you're already doing, you'll notice a real difference in how you handle your long-term problems.

It might surprise you to know that lots of apparently confident people employ techniques – 'tricks' if you like – to get them through difficult situations. And you can learn some of these too.

You must believe that you have low self-esteem, or you wouldn't have bought this book and stuck with it thus far. But it doesn't necessarily follow that you feel isolated or lonely. If you don't, you can just skim this chapter, or maybe skip it altogether.

However, if you feel that you never seem to have enough friends, or that you find it difficult to get close to people, then the information in this chapter will help you.

In fact, what I'm going to do in the next few pages is to try to show you how we often put potential friends off by how we look and act. And then I'm going to highlight what makes people *like* people. Lastly, I'm going to discuss friendship – and how it works best.

Poor self-esteem, isolation and how we appear to others

Many people with poor self-esteem feel quite isolated. Women, in particular, often have plenty of school, college/university and work friends, but then lose touch with this network while they're bringing up their children.

This isn't quite so damaging if they replace old friends with new ones – probably other women with children of roughly the same age as their own. But if they don't, they can end up feeling pretty lonely.

Anna is a typical example. She's now fifty-two and is finding life very tough. Anna has low self-esteem. This is largely due to the fact that her mother – a lone parent – was a businesswoman who never had much time for her daughter in the week, and who took to her bed with migraines at the weekends. I sometimes think Anna brought herself up, as she seems to have had no parenting from her mother at all.

As in many of these situations, the saving grace in the household was the granny, who loved Anna very much. But when her grandmother died, Anna felt totally bereft.

As a child, Anna had *some* friends, but because her mother was always busy, or in bed feeling poorly, she was never able to invite other children home. She felt inhibited with her peers because of her mother; so much so that she often deliberately stopped herself from getting close to people.

As an adult, Anna worked for the United Nations and travelled a great deal. She had work colleagues, but no real close friends. Then she met Tom. He was a larger-than-life character – very blustery and driven. He seemed impressed by her quietness and her intelligence and culture – and, much to everyone's surprise, the two of them married.

Tom – and later three daughters – became Anna's life. Unfortunately, her marriage didn't have much going for it. Tom was mad on golf and rugby while she was interested in chamber music. She loved travelling in Europe, he favoured America. It wasn't long before Tom started having affairs, and although he always provided for Anna very well financially, there was little love or companionship in their partnership.

For Anna, who had had little love in her life, the thought of starting again and being single was terrifying. So although the marriage wasn't great, she figured that it was better than nothing – and probably all she deserved anyway – so she kept quiet about how she was treated and soldiered on with the relationship.

Eventually, Tom left her – as she had always suspected he would. This made her feel even more worthless. And because she didn't have many friends before the marriage, and made few during it – and her children have now grown up and gone away – she is lonely. Not only that, she has lost the knack – if she ever had it – of making friends.

She often said to me: 'I don't really have any friends.' This phrase sounded very hollow and hopeless and I felt that what she was really saying was: 'No one likes me.'

Now, Anna is actually a very cultured, attractive and warm

woman. But unfortunately, because of her lack of self-regard – which has been reinforced by a difficult marriage and also by having too few friends – she's built a bit of an emotional shell around herself, so that she looks rather self-contained. Not only that, she can appear rather haughty, critical and unfriendly.

This has proved to be a big problem, because people don't tend to respond to her well at a first meeting – and so it is very difficult for her to make new friends.

Some people reading this book will identify with a situation where shyness and poor self-esteem make you retreat into yourself and appear to be arrogant or unfriendly. In fact, I used to be like it myself.

When I was a very unhappy seventeen-year-old with virtually no confidence and lousy self-esteem, I didn't communicate well with people at all. Looking back, I realise I never thought about how I affected other people. Probably I assumed that they didn't notice me.

So it was a complete shock one day to be told by my head mistress – who was a really lovely lady and a big help to me – that I looked unapproachable and aloof, and that people thought I was looking down on them.

Me? Looking down on *them*? When my own life was such a mess! I didn't think I could be hearing her right. But apparently she'd had a complaint from a new teacher, who felt that I treated her with contempt.

Frankly, I now believe that this complaint spoke volumes about the teacher's lack of self-esteem! Nonetheless, I learned a valuable lesson from it. I realised what an impact one's expression can have on someone else – and how easily it can be misinterpreted. It also occurred to me, for the very first time, that just because someone was older than me, it didn't mean they were brimming with confidence. In fact, I began to understand that they might have less than me – and here was I thinking that *I'd* got the monopoly on shyness and awkwardness!

Now, it could be that you have tended to go through life thinking that everyone else is more confident and able than you. And also that you have failed to realise that your face and your body language may be responsible for your lack of a social life. So, let's try to change all that.

Nowadays, it's very easy to see for yourself how you appear to other people. You may well catch a glimpse of your image in a grimy train window, or in a mirror in a shop, or even on a CCTV monitor. What do you look like in that split second before you pull your tummy in or hold your head a little higher?

Don't stop to worry about your hair, or whether you're carrying a few pounds too many. It's your face and general demeanour you should be interested in.

You might be rather shattered to find that you look like your mum on a bad day! Or angry, haughty, arrogant, dowdy, stressed out, chaotic, or very uninterested in other people.

Remember that this is exactly what other people see when they encounter you. Is this how you *want* to come across to others? If not, you need to work at portraying a more positive image.

I suggest you try to *feel* when your face has hardened into a moody, cross, critical, or unfriendly mask. If you can develop an awareness of how your face looks by what it *feels* like, you'll be able to stop yourself from appearing unapproachable. Off-putting expressions can become habitual and make you look older than you are. But even worse than this, they stop people from wanting to get to know you. Become aware of what your face is telling people. And if you discover that you're looking less than your bright and happy best, try this little trick:

Conjure up a vision of something that you know will lighten your expression. This can be a bowl of your favourite-flavour ice cream. Or it might be your child's first smile. Or a memory of what your partner looked like when the two of you fell in love. Whatever it is, your expression will change into a much pleasanter one. Be aware of what is happening to your face. Feel how you raise your head, so that you stop looking downwards. Sense how your eyes widen and take on a softer expression; how your cheekbones lift, how your mouth moistens and how the corners of your lips start curling upwards. You might even go the whole hog and *smile*!

This technique will help you to look much more open and inviting. Try practising it in front of the mirror. You'll feel silly at first. But that will make you laugh – which is no bad thing.

My friend and fellow therapist, Ian Claffey, always tells his clients to concentrate on smiling when they meet someone for the first time. As he so wisely says: 'You don't get two chances to make a good first impression.'

Now, you might think that smiling is overrated or a bit of a cliché in this situation, but the fact is that it opens hearts and minds. It always has and it always will. If you don't smile easily, try practising – in front of that mirror. A genuine, warm smile is worth a thousand charming words.

How you look when you meet people for the first time

Some people who grow to become great friends or even lovers don't actually *like* each other at a first meeting. But they're in the minority. Mostly, we have the chance to make new friends when an initial meeting goes well. And if you are someone who feels that your poor self-esteem holds you back in terms of meeting people and making new friends, you should try to ensure that as many individuals as possible warm to you when they first meet you. This will encourage them to want to know you better. And feeling liked and wanted is *great* for our self-esteem habit.

Some people instinctively seem to know how to relate to others. But most of us have to learn these skills. And so if you tend to be a bit unsure of yourself in company, but you tell yourself that it's easy for everyone else, please think again. The chances are that many individuals who you think are good at making an initial contact have actually had to work at it.

So, what do most people look for when they meet someone new?

Recently, I conducted a mini-survey where I asked two hundred adults what qualities they look for when they meet someone for the very first time.

In a moment, I'll list these qualities for you, but first here are a few comments from some of those I surveyed:

Peter, a popular local politician, says of a first meeting with someone: 'I look for things like smiles and eyes: windows of the soul and all that! Clean fingernails don't hurt. Handshakes seem to sort out the also-rans very quickly. And bad teeth and bad breath are totally off-putting.'

So, a mixture of welcoming body language and good personal hygiene does it for him.

Tina, a journalist, warms to a twinkle in the eye. 'An obvious sense of humour, and some indication of kindness and sensitivity is also vital,' she says. 'Liking animals is a good pointer. And I like to feel that someone values him or herself, but that there is some vulnerability there too.'

And Susan, a fifty-something divorcée who has made a new career for herself since her marriage broke up, lists eye contact, good manners, warmth, openness and enthusiasm as attractive qualities in new contacts. But she is seriously turned-off by aloofness, lack of eye contact, insensitivity, arrogance and a lack of personal cleanliness.

Mandy, a PR consultant, is drawn to men and women who are empathetic, interested in others, funny and liberal. But she hates individuals who are too self-interested, bossy, aggressive or very religious.

Melanie, a young mother, tells me that she tends to warm to other young mothers – because of everything they have in common. But she greatly dislikes adults who appear to talk down to her, or who don't listen to what she has to say.

Top fifteen turn-ons at first meeting

I asked two hundred people the question: 'What do you look for when you meet a person for the very first time?'

And these are the qualities they came up with. In other words, these are the things *about* people that make other people want to know them:

- sense of humour
- enthusiastic and outward going
- friendly
- good eye contact
- nice smile and/or pleasant facial expression
- interest in person they're talking to
- chatty
- good listener
- genuine
- mutual interests
- nice looking
- intelligent
- polite
- smells nice
- good dress sense

Top fifteen turn-offs at first meeting

And these were the top fifteen turn-offs. People do not respond well to individuals who are:

- too confident
- uninterested in the person they're talking to
- insincere
- arrogant
- rude
- unable or reluctant to make eye contact
- offensive because of poor personal hygiene: bad teeth and smelly breath are total turn-offs
- loud
- boring, or who have a boring voice
- too serious
- unfriendly
- lazy – and don't seem to want to bother to converse
- too serious

- aggressive
- narrow-minded

These results show very clearly that what most folk respond well to in a first meeting are characteristics such as humour, enthusiasm, friendliness, good eye contact, a smiling face and so on. These are things we can all work on.

Interestingly, loads of individuals with poor self-esteem tell me that they don't do well in company because they're not hugely intelligent, because they're not great looking, because they don't exude confidence, or because they don't have particularly nice clothes. And yet, as you can see, these particular characteristics come very low down on the list compared with qualities such as friendliness and sincerity.

Clearly, if you want to come across as the very decent, kind person you are, you need to focus on being interested and friendly – and in smiling and looking someone in the eye.

And what do you want to avoid?

Well, you don't want to appear over-confident. That's for sure – as it puts people's backs up. Now, people with poor self-esteem don't often come across as over-confident, but sometimes they *do* if they're trying too hard. So this is something to watch out for.

Obviously, it's also crucial to be genuine and interested in those you meet. In other words if you can develop an attitude which comes across as genuinely warm, most individuals will warm to you.

I can't imagine that anyone reading this book needs to be reminded about issues of personal hygiene. But of course there are adults with poor self-esteem who are also phobic about dentists – and if this should apply to you, do remember that an unhealthy mouth breeds germs, decay and odour. And bad breath is a turn-off that virtually every one of my respondents mentioned.

Nowadays, there are masses of good dentists skilled in helping adults who are terrified of dental treatment. Some use hypnosis, or other relaxation methods – and they get very good results. So if you haven't been to a dentist for years because you're frightened, why not make this the month when you seek help?

Ring round a few local practices, and ask if one of the partners specialises in nervous patients. It shouldn't take you long to find one.

Meanwhile, make sure you use a mouthwash and dental floss daily. They're good for your dental health – and essential if you're going to be someone that others want to know.

Making friends and keeping them

So now you have a good idea of what makes people *like* other people – and you can work at perfecting those skills that are attractive to others. The next step, then, is to look at the whole question of friendship.

Why do some people have loads of friends while others find it difficult to get any, or to keep the ones they have?

How to make new friends

The simple answer is that they play the numbers game. It's only in television commercials that a fascinating new neighbour comes round to borrow some coffee. Mostly, we have to get out of the house in order to find new friends.

The best way to achieve this, in my opinion, is to meet people who have similar interests to your own. So if you're into yoga, don't do it at home with a video – join a class.

If you're learning French, don't do it by correspondence course – go to an evening class. If you have a naughty puppy, go and walk him in the park where lots of other dog-owners congregate, and ask their opinion on how to handle him.

This kind of approach may sound like common sense – which it is – but you'd be amazed at the number of adults who pursue the same routine day in, day out, year in, year out, even though it does not offer them the chance to meet new people. New contacts are potential new friends.

Keeping up with the friends you have

If you have friends, but you don't see them often enough, then you have to make a conscious effort to fit them into your lives.

It's a good idea to go through your address book twice a year, and to make a list of the pals that you never seem to see but who you'd really like to be in touch with. Then *get* in touch. Just do it. Phone them, or e-mail them. Have a good chat and – most important of all – if it's humanly possible, arrange to meet.

Of course, from time to time you're going to encounter some rejection, because your call may coincide with a time when your friend is moving house, or is not well, or is having a rough time at work, or trying to hold a marriage together. But the important thing is that you've made the effort. And if you get into the habit of doing this, you'll find that you start seeing a lot more of the people who matter to you.

Balance in friendship

Friendship depends on a sharing of information and confidences: a sort of emotional give and take, if you like.

Unfortunately, many people with poor self-esteem don't offer enough of themselves. This is almost as unhelpful as being totally self-obsessed.

To be a good friend to someone, you need to be able to talk about yourself and to admit when you're down, or when you need some help.

If you don't, other people will feel that you're keeping them at arm's length or that you don't trust them.

If you know that you're a good listener and a kind of agony aunt for your friends, that's great – but don't adopt this role all of the time. If you do, you'll find that nice friends will feel shut out by your attitude, and that nastier folk will take advantage of you.

Lastly, don't forget that you *deserve* friends. If you're not sure that you believe me, then you need to do more work on challenging your Negative Inner Commentaries.

And if – despite the advice and information in this chapter – you believe that you're never going to be able to make more friends because you're too shy, then the next chapter is especially for you.

8

Deal with Your Shyness – and Improve Your Self-Esteem

Are there people on this earth who are never, ever shy? There may be, but I don't think I've met any.

Moderate shyness is certainly something most of us claim to feel on occasions. It's not awful. It's normal. And frequently, other people find it quite endearing.

The boyfriend of a popular TV actress told me about being alone with his partner: 'She looks so confident on the box, or when she's meeting the public,' he said. 'But in private, when she's not acting, and not being a "celeb", she's quite shy – and I find it enormously attractive.'

He's not alone. Men find a certain amount of shyness a bit of a turn on. They especially like blushing – which is the bane of many a young woman's life. The reason for this is probably unconscious, but it's very powerful because it's all about sex!

You see, when a woman is having sex and she's approaching orgasm she usually develops a distinct flush on her face, neck and breasts.

So when a man sees a woman blushing he is often instinctively drawn to her because he interprets the blushing as a sign of arousal. This is something to think about if you're someone who blushes easily and you're very worried about it: maybe it's not such a bad thing after all!

As for shy men – men who are terrified that no woman will ever look at them because they're quiet and sensitive and not loud and macho like their mates – well, the truth is that masses of women find them enormously appealing, sweet, unthreatening and sexy.

But there are degrees of shyness. So far I've been writing about the kind where you might feel nervous about walking into a party, starting a new job, or going on a first date. This is all pretty average stuff – and a good way to deal with it is to realise that most other people feel exactly the same way.

But at the other end of the scale there's the sort of acute shyness that can cripple people emotionally and socially, and seriously inhibit their enjoyment of life. And I know that many readers of this book will suffer from it.

The other day I read an article which said that one woman was so shy she was unable to shout 'House' at a Bingo game. Unbelievably, because she couldn't find her voice, she missed out on a prize of £90,000. That's an extreme example of real, desperate and inhibiting shyness.

Now, the trouble is that unlike a sprained ankle, or a cold, or a spot on your chin, extreme shyness won't clear up on its own. Not real, gut-wrenching shyness. The reason for this of course is that the shy person needs to face – not avoid – the situations that he or she is frightened of. Most seriously shy people *don't* face these situations; they go through life trying very hard to avoid them.

Social phobias

You may have heard of the term 'social phobia'. This is a kind of shyness which is debilitating and deeply stressful, but which is usually limited to specific situations.

Some people with social phobias can't eat when they're with other people. Others can't take a drink in public because their hands shake so violently. A few have panic attacks if they have to sign their name with anyone watching them.

This kind of problem can be helped by the measures outlined in this book, but, at its worst, it may need specialist treatment in the form of behaviour or cognitive psychotherapy.

Drugs

Many shy people believe that their only hope of feeling more confident is to take some kind of drug.

Tranquillisers used to be prescribed for shyness, before it was commonly realised how addictive they were. In fact, some doctors dished them out like Smarties. But did these pills cure the problem? No, they didn't.

Nowadays, most experts believe that tranquillisers should be restricted to very occasional use – for instance, if you have to address a conference once a year and you're terrified of public speaking.

Rare usage of this kind can help individuals get through something that is causing them great anxiety. But it doesn't actually cure the person; it just gives him or her a bit of pharmaceutical support. We now know that it's dangerous to give this support too often – because it only leads to a dependency, which can be even more of a problem than the original shyness.

But we're not just talking prescription drugs here. Many shy people have tried leisure drugs of various kinds to diminish shyness. And practically everyone at some time or another has resorted to drugging themselves with alcohol for a bit of 'Dutch' courage.

But drugs can only dull the sense of anxiety. Usually, the shy person needs more and more of this 'dulling down' as time goes on. So drugs don't solve shyness, they just damp it down. If you really want to sort out your shyness once and for all you have to find another way.

Skills for a more confident life

Another method is to learn new skills. These will take time, patience and energy. But if you're prepared to work at them, your new skills will become automatic behaviour and they'll increase your habit of good self-esteem dramatically – because the more you overcome your shyness, the better you'll feel about yourself.

Shyness can occur in all sorts of areas. But the commonest are to do with social gatherings and meeting new people. The rest of this chapter is devoted to hints and tips that will be useful in these situations – because if we can master these, we can carry our new-found confidence into dealing with our personal relationships, friendships, family and work.

(i) Use of role models

This is quite a jolly skill to work on. It often helps one to cope with difficult situations if you imagine how someone you admire would behave in such circumstances. This takes your mind off yourself – and your supposed inadequacies.

I have a shy, male client, who finds it easier to walk into a roomful of strangers if he pretends that he's the elegant former cricketer, David Gower.

This kind of play-acting can be really beneficial. In fact, if you begin by acting, in the end you may well find that your behaviour in these situations becomes accomplished and automatic.

Can you think of someone who, in your view, would rarely put a foot wrong? Someone you could use as a good example to follow? Someone you could model yourself on at a party, on a first date, when you meet your prospective in-laws, on the first day of a new job, or when you have to do jury service?

Here are some women who, I believe, make ideal role models, but you may want to pick someone entirely different:

Joanna Lumley
Lisa Tarbuck
Clare Short
Diane Abbot
Anna Ford

And, if you're male, one of the following may fit the bill:

Jeremy Paxman
Neil Pearson
Trevor McDonald
Sean Connery
Gary Lineker
Des Lynam

It doesn't matter whom you pick, so long as they appear confident and happy in their own skin. But do avoid celebrities who've got difficulties with drink or drugs – they've probably got more problems than you!

Your selected person should be someone you can look up to at all times. And he or she certainly doesn't have to be in the public eye: you might want to pick a past school teacher, a boss you've liked, or a relative. That's fine, as long as their image is a strong one for you so that when you're nervous you're instantly able to visualise them – and imitate their behaviour.

(ii) Stop making assumptions – unless you've got a crystal ball

A lot of people with poor self-regard make false assumptions about others – especially when they're meeting people for the first time.

'She wouldn't want to talk to me,' we say. Or: 'I know he would find me boring.'

Well, unless you've got a crystal ball, how can you possibly know in advance what someone is going to decide about you?

Plenty of individuals, who you might think of as too attractive or successful to be interested in you, are actually quite shy themselves. And they may even feel rather neglected at social gatherings because the rest of us are too busy feeling inadequate and hesitant about going up and speaking to them.

So, if you're at the office party, or on a course, or at a conference, or even just at a friend's house and you'd like to make the acquaintance of someone who – in your opinion – is actually out of your league, why not speak to this person? It may go well. And if doesn't, then at least you've had a bit of a practice that might reap rewards another time.

(iii) Talk to five new people a day

This is a good exercise for a person who never speaks unless spoken to. The fact is that if we never initiate a conversation, people can think we're stand-offish rather than just shy. And while we're assuming that the other person should speak first, we're forgetting that he or she might be just as timid as we are – if not more so. This is how golden opportunities for friendship and romance are missed.

Get into the habit of routinely talking to new people – and then when you really, really want to talk to someone new at a party or at work, you'll find you've got the skill to do it.

One way of getting through your daily quota of new people is to tackle it first thing in the morning by saying 'hello' to five people on your bus, or at the railway station. In this way, some individuals will become your 'regulars' – and you'll start greeting them without much effort every time you meet them. You might even make a friend of one or two of them. But don't stop there: to keep improving, you need to find five *new* people every day.

In no time, you'll find you're gaining the reputation of being 'that friendly woman' or 'that charming gentleman'. And you'll feel proud of yourself that you're putting yourself out this way. You'll also sense – from their responses – that you're brightening other people's days, and this will add to your growing sense of worth and affirmation.

I do realise that what I'm asking will feel like a terrifying task for some of my readers. But the fact is that it's not impossible. Not for anyone. And with each day it'll get easier – and after a while it won't seem a chore. In fact, you may even grow to like it.

(iv) If you go to a social gathering – try something different

What are you like at a party? Do you look at the ground? Are you defensive? Or do you talk too much in your shyness?

Try to analyse how you normally behave – and then decide on another approach.

If you normally chatter away, decide to think before speaking and to do rather more listening than you normally do.

If you tend to only talk to people you know, or to stand alone, make a big effort to walk up to someone you'd normally never speak to: someone you don't think looks your type of person at all. Say 'Hello', tell them your name, offer your hand. And see what happens.

The chances are that by breaking a pattern, you'll feel and act differently from normal – and you'll have more fun.

(v) Relax

Whenever you're going to tackle a situation that is likely to make you nervous, whether it's a job interview, meeting some friends in a pub, going on a first date, or speaking up in class, take time to get yourself as relaxed as possible before you go.

Yoga, self-hypnosis, or meditation are all good methods. But if you're not adept at any of these, just buy yourself a relaxation tape. Many chemists and health-food shops sell them. And there are details of one particular brand in the Help Yourself Guide at the end of the book.

(vi) Talk about what you know

Sometimes, when we're ill at ease, we make the mistake of talking about topics we know nothing about. We might hear ourselves –

desperate to impress – say: 'What on earth are we going to do about Kashmir?'

Or we try to sound convincing about the Premier League, or the rating of local schools, or whether or not to join the Euro, when we don't know a lot about any of them. This kind of pretence is not going to help you – in fact, it'll make you more nervous. Stick to what you know. Imagine Joanna Lumley, or David Gower in that situation. Would they pretend? I don't think so. They'd probably just move off to talk to someone else, or laugh and say that they can't contribute much to the conversation as they don't know enough about it.

So don't feel you're stupid or inept just because you're not an expert on everything! And if anyone asks you a question directly about something you haven't a clue about – then admit it. Pause. Smile. And say: 'I'm the last person you should ask about that because I really don't know. But you can explain it to me, if you like. I'm a keen student!'

As a general rule, when you meet someone new, begin by keeping the conversation very simple. Find out if you have mutual friends. Enquire if the other person has seen a film you recently enjoyed. Compliment the person you're talking to. Comments like 'Great tie!', or: 'That top is a great colour for you', are friendly, and are very pleasant to receive.

And if *you* are complimented, accept the remarks with grace. Don't argue.

There is nothing more off-putting for someone than having a compliment cast back in his or her face. Never forget that the person you're talking to may be just as shy as you are – and may be devastated by your response.

So if someone says: 'Your hair is lovely', smile and say 'Thanks.' Don't say: 'It needs cutting', or: 'I couldn't get it right tonight.' This implies that the other person's judgement isn't up to much. You may think you're just being modest, but the chances are you'll sound rude.

(vii) Personal space

People who are completely at ease with other people seem to know instinctively how close they should get to another individual. But when we're nervous it's easy to get it wrong. We might stand too far away, so we're inaudible and not able to 'connect'. Or, in our anxiety, we may stand too close. In the UK, it's normal to stand about two feet away from someone we're talking to but don't know well. Obviously, if the party is very crowded or noisy, we may have to stand closer. But as a general rule, less than two feet feels too close, and more than four feet away feels too remote.

(viii) Open questions

When I was a young television reporter and presenter, I quickly learned that some questions guarantee useful answers, while others don't.

My first ever interview was with a tense and uncommunicative Norfolk farmer. It was diabolical. I asked a lot of questions beginning my sentences with: 'What . . .', 'Do you . . .', and 'Is . . .'. And I quickly discovered that when you do that, a difficult interviewee is likely to respond with one-word answers.

'What's your main crop?' I asked.

'Onions,' he replied.

'Do you like farming?'

'No.'

'Is this a good year for onions?'

'No.'

'Do you sell directly to the public?'

'Yup.'

'Is it possible for them to Pick Their Own?'

'Yes.'

I certainly didn't cover myself with glory *that* day! I'd made the mistake of using 'Closed Questions' – to which people can virtually end the conversation with one word.

But I soon learned that if you use the words 'how' or 'why' to start a question, you're likely to get much better responses, because an answer is always going to involve more than one word. Questions that begin 'How . . .' or 'Why . . .' are called 'Open Questions', and these are the sort of questions you should try to use when you're instigating a conversation – particularly with someone you don't know. Don't say: 'Did you come by bus?' Because you'll probably get a one-word answer back. Instead say: 'How did you get here this evening?'

Admittedly, such a question *can* be answered in two words, such as: 'By car', or 'By bus'. But the chances are that the other person will jump at the chance to tell you how difficult it is to get a bus at that time of the evening, or will give you a blow-by-blow account of the traffic on the North Circular.

Of course, this might not be the most fascinating conversation you've ever had, but it will break the ice.

(ix) Have a practice

If social gatherings are really difficult for you, have a practice before you go. Use your mirror at home to see how you look. Rehearse smiling at new people. Look your image right in the eye. This is vitally important. Even if you're desperately shy, always try to look someone in the eye when you first meet. As you learned in the last chapter, eye contact at a first meeting is highly rated by people. It indicates interest and makes others more likely to respond positively to you.

Also, practise a few greetings. Use a tape recorder if possible, to hear how you sound. Do you sound bright and inviting? Yes? Good. That's what you want.

And before you leave the house, draw up a list of three questions you can use in order to get conversations going that evening.

There's nothing wrong with rehearsing. You'd be amazed at how many people rehearse what they're going to say on a date, or at the office 'do' or at the PTA meeting. Having some idea of how you're going to start conversations gives you confidence.

(x) Deep breathing and distraction techniques

I know a very good actress who gets sick with nerves before a performance. She feels panicky, her heart races, and her palms sweat. These are the very same symptoms that many shy people experience in social situations.

My actress friend gets over her problem by taking five deep breaths and by completely exhaling between each one. This has a very calming effect, so when you're very nervous, why not give it a go?

It's also helpful to distract yourself in some way. One man I know wears a tight elastic band round his right wrist and when he's feeling panicky he surreptitiously twangs the elastic band so that it really hurts. While he's concentrating on the sudden stinging pain in his right wrist, he's not thinking about how nervous he feels.

A woman I know feels very 'trembly' at parties and has terrible anxieties about what she believes is a visible shaking in her hands. So, when she's talking to someone and is feeling really nervous, she distracts herself by pressing her left foot really hard into the ground. She uses a lot of force, but no one else can see what she's doing. Her whole focus is on weighing down that foot. And, because her body is busy exerting all that pressure, she forgets her hands – and of course then they don't shake.

Mirroring

Have you noticed how often people feel comfortable with other people with whom they have things in common? Often a couple will have come together because they share a love of music, or two people who both have dogs will have loads to chat about.

When you're trying to talk to people and to make friends, try to establish common ground. But, as well as finding common interests or mutual friends, you can engender a feeling of sameness and comfort by use of body language. This will make the other person feel more at home with you.

Try to mirror the other person's behaviour. If you're sitting chatting, watch how the other person is sitting. And rearrange yourself so that you're sitting in a similar way. If he is leaning backwards, in a relaxed manner, try to be more relaxed yourself. If he is sitting forward, looking very enthusiastic, try to do the same. Then, if, for example, you're both enjoying a cup of coffee, you can sip from your drink at the same time as the other person does. This helps the atmosphere to become more easy. And if things progress to a romantic stage, it will increase the intimacy if you time your breathing to match that of the other person!

This mirroring will give you something to concentrate on, instead of your shyness. It will also stop you fidgeting – a common problem when one is nervous – which can make other people feel uneasy. And it will encourage the other person to feel comfortable in your company.

(xi) Self-disclosure

When you meet someone new, things are unlikely to go well unless there's an exchange of chat.

Now, as a shy person you may well have learned how to be a good listener, and this particular skill may have got you through many worrying social situations. But if you're to progress beyond the point where people think you're 'nice' to the point where they really want to know you better or to become your friend, you really need to offer information about yourself as well as listening to others.

This is very hard for some shy people. In fact, I know one guy who finds it difficult to even say what he does for a living! And the strange thing is that he has a very good job.

So, don't forget to offer little titbits about yourself. If the other person has talked about her recent bout of 'flu and then asks if you've had it, don't just say 'No.' Instead, come up with an answer that tells the other person something about you. You might say: 'Actually, I seem to be very lucky. I never get colds or 'flu, but that may be because I've started taking zinc every day.'

Or you might say: 'I'm sorry you had 'flu. It sounds horrid. Actually, I had a couple of days off work because I felt off-colour, but, thankfully, it didn't develop into anything nasty. Have you ever thought about having a 'flu jab?'

This kind of exchange is not easy for a shy person, but with practice it becomes easier – and it will make a huge difference to your social confidence.

(xii) Breaking old rules

Lots of us have old rules that don't help us. For example, you may have been taught that it's polite not to speak till you're spoken to. But if you keep this rule, you can go through whole evenings without saying a word.

You may have been taught never to interrupt people, but if you're at a party where everyone else is busy chatting when you arrive, you'll have a pretty lonely existence if you don't interrupt *someone*.

Have a think about what holds you back. Is it a rule that you're holding on to? If so, break it now and again – and you'll realise that the world doesn't come to an end. You might also find it has very positive results for you.

(xiii) Drawing attention to yourself

Many shy people would almost sooner die than draw attention to themselves. But it's this inhibition which is causing them to remain shy – and often lonely and unfulfilled too.

If you know this applies to you, try drawing attention to yourself once a day. You can start with small things like wearing something unusual to work, or asking someone to bring you back a coffee – when you would normally sooner go thirsty than ask this kind of favour.

But once you've mastered this kind of situation, try progressing to something that makes you blush just to think of it. What about upsetting a glass of water in a café? Or sending back a meal in a restaurant because it's not hot enough? Or, when you're on a crowded train and the ticket collector comes round to check tickets, pluck up courage to make a complaint about the dirty state of the compartment, and ask for his assurance that he'll pass on your complaint to the train company.

Once you can tackle these sorts of embarrassing tasks and realise that the ceiling doesn't cave in, and that you have a right to draw attention to yourself – even get things wrong or make a fool of yourself – then you'll feel wonderfully liberated.

And – most importantly of all – you'll improve your levels of self-esteem.

9

Assertiveness: How to Say What You Mean and Mean What You Say – Calmly

Are you someone who doesn't say what you want to say? Is it difficult for you to say 'no'? Do you tend to keep quiet when you should be speaking up for yourself? Do you sometimes go straight from saying nothing to erupting with a fury that surprises you and everyone around you?

Well, these are tendencies of people who don't value themselves enough.

Masses of people with poor self-esteem are too passive. And quite a lot of them are too aggressive – on occasions. But the ideal to aim for is to be *assertive*.

If you are assertive, you are able to stand up for yourself and your rights without resorting to anger. If you don't think you can do that at present, then this chapter is especially for you.

You are, in fact, already working towards becoming more assertive, by identifying your Negative Inner Commentaries and changing them into Positive Inner Commentaries. But in the next few pages, we're going to look at how you can learn to appear more assertive by changing your behaviour.

If you're not assertive, you'll frequently feel out of control

People who don't value themselves much find it very difficult indeed to be assertive. They often keep very quiet when they should be putting their own point of view across, or saying what they believe to be right, or standing up for themselves.

Unfortunately, when they *don't* speak up at an appropriate time, they tend to get all hot and bothered inside. Then they start simmering with anger, and if they *still* don't speak their mind, they're likely to erupt, like a pan boiling over.

This is often quite terrifying for them – and totally amazing for everyone else. And it rarely helps them to get their point across – instead, it encourages other people to dismiss their ranting as 'hysterical'.

I've lost count of the number of times a client has confessed to me that she completely lost control over an issue that had been getting to her for a long time.

'I didn't know myself,' one woman said to me. 'I went completely berserk. I could see red-hot pokers in front of my eyes. I think I could have killed in that moment. I went totally over the top. I threw things. I used swear words I didn't know I knew. I thought I was actually going completely mad.'

Was this woman's anger justified? It certainly was. She had a partner who had been cheating on her for years but who had always maintained that all the signs and signals of his affair were her imagination. He also managed to persuade her that she was a bit 'neurotic' and that maybe she should 'see a psychiatrist' because she was obviously 'paranoid'. Finally, she caught him in bed with another woman – and she flew into a wild rage.

So, yes, my client was angry and had a right to be so. But it actually did not help her cause at all to be swamped with aggression in that way. It upset her a great deal and it did nothing to sort the situation – except to give her old man a bit of a shock.

Passive anger

We all get angry from time to time, but we can be much more effective in making a point if we deal with our grievance assertively long before we get to the aggressive stage. Unfortunately, many individuals with poor self-esteem don't have the necessary skills to do that.

So what tends to happen is that when they start to get angry, they go into a routine to 'show' their anger rather than express it calmly. They sigh heavily. They refuse to meet anyone else's eye. They drum their fingers on the table. They bang around the house or office, tidying things away – noisily. And if they're asked if something is wrong, they either don't answer, or they grunt, or they sigh again and say: 'Nothing.'

This is 'passive' anger. Frankly, the way we behave when we're passively angry just makes us appear rather silly. And no one responds well to it.

I've got a friend, Monica, whose widowed mother drops round to her home rather too frequently.

One day her mother rang Monica at work and said: 'I'll pop round this evening and have a drink and a gossip with you.'

Monica sighed heavily down the phone. She also started drumming her fingers on the desk – which was a wasted gesture as her mum couldn't see or hear it.

'Anything wrong, love?' asked her mother.

'No – oo.'

'I thought you sounded a bit fed up?'

Now this was the cue for Monica to say: 'Sorry, Mum. Please don't come round tonight. I've got other plans.'

But of course her mother was not going to pick up on that unless it was said very firmly, because she was lonely, and the easiest way for her to while away an evening was with her daughter.

So Monica listened to her Mum saying: 'I thought you sounded a bit fed up', and instead of coming out with the truth, she heard herself reply: 'Oh, it's nothing. I think my work's getting me down.'

So her mother then said: 'Oh, well, in that case, I'll cook you a meal when I come round then, shall I?'

Monica groaned inwardly. But she said nothing, hoping that somehow the whole situation would just go away.

Aggressive anger

If you don't make your point assertively, you're likely to go into a passive anger phase, just like Monica. And, if no one picks up on your signals during the passive anger phase, you will progress to the next stage – *aggressive* anger. And that's what happened to Monica.

By the time that her mother turned up at Monica's house that night, armed with a big bag of groceries, Monica had worked herself into a right old lather and could barely be civil to her parent. After they'd bumped into each other in the small kitchen a couple of times, Monica was so angry that she lost her temper with her mother.

'You're living your life through me,' she stormed. 'You don't let me have any time to myself – and you never seem to think I might want to see my friends. All I wanted was a quiet night – but could you let me have it? Oh no. You're so selfish you don't notice when I'm trying to hint that I could do with some peace and quiet. You make me sick!'

Not surprisingly, Monica's mum swept up her things and left, banging the door behind her. They didn't speak again for over three weeks – during which time they were both miserable.

If Monica had had the skills to be assertive, none of this would have happened.

The assertive way is the best way

So, don't be a Monica. If you know you tend to act like she does, try to find your voice. Be calm. Be pleasant. Be firm. Say: 'I'd rather you didn't come over, Mum, not tonight. I need a few hours on my own to get some chores done. I'll phone you tomorrow and fix another day.'

Can you see that by speaking out early you can avoid a lot of pain? There's a skill to this and it will get better with practice. But try to remember these things:

- Make your point earlier rather than later.
- You have the right to say 'no'.
- Take a deep breath before you make your point.
- Lower the volume of your voice and the pitch of it. You can do this by thinking of your voice as a long, purple velvet ribbon that flows gracefully downwards out of your mouth. As you speak, imagine your voice following the downward curve of that richly coloured velvet. Think low-pitched. Think firm. Think clear. Think low-volume. This is important, particularly if you're female, because it's common for people who don't want to hear what a woman has to say to accuse her of being shrill or hysterical. It's nearly always men who do this – but some women do it too. If you do become loud, or too high pitched, this will play into the hands of such individuals. So practise being assertive, not aggressive – and keep your voice low in pitch and low in volume (this does NOT mean inaudible!). When you do, you'll notice that people take you much more seriously.

You'll sound more assertive if you start your sentences with the word 'I'

If you want to make a point assertively, you should make liberal use of the word 'I'. So you'll say:

- 'I would rather you didn't come round tonight.'
- 'I need a few hours on my own.'
- 'I will phone you tomorrow.'

This is an important little technique. When we start to get angry we commonly use the word 'you'. As in:

- 'You're living your life through me.'
- 'You don't let me have any time to myself.'
- 'You're selfish.'
- 'You make me sick.'

These statements beginning with 'you' are not likely to achieve your aims without someone feeling angry or put down. They sound aggressive and accusatory – and on the whole individuals on the receiving end of this kind of treatment won't like it. In fact they'll almost certainly get angry themselves – and you won't achieve what you want.

So speak early. Speak calmly. Keep your voice low in volume and pitch. And make your point using the word 'I'.

But perhaps a good row would clear the air?

I personally do not subscribe to the view that a good row clears the air. For many people, aggressive anger is very upsetting. And when we go into that kind of state we often dredge up things that we don't mean. Worse still we frequently come out with things that are much better left unsaid.

When we are calmly assertive – as opposed to aggressively angry – we can make a point without being destructive, without demolishing the other person and his or her point of view – and without bringing stuff which is totally irrelevant into the situation.

Giving and taking criticism

The whole area of criticism is especially difficult for people with a poor self-esteem habit. I actually know people who have refused to go for a promotion because the new job would involve them in having to be a boss, and therefore having – from time to time – to criticise someone.

Now, I'm not saying that everyone should be ambitious, or that you're a failure if you don't seek promotion. There are always going to be individuals who've decided that they want a quieter life than a boss might have, and that they want plenty of time for leisure, friends and family outside work. These are perfectly valid reasons for not seeking too much career advancement.

But if you feel you can't apply for a better job simply because you'd be terrified of having to tell people what to do, and of having to reprimand them if the occasion demanded it, then that's a pretty barmy reason for holding yourself back. Because you *can* learn how to handle people, and you can certainly learn how to give constructive criticism.

In a nutshell, the art of good and fair criticism is to use the assertive skills already outlined in this chapter – speak using low-pitch and low-volume, speak calmly and firmly, and use statements beginning with the word 'I'.

It also helps if you preface any criticism by offering some praise first. You might say: 'Derek, I think you did a marvellous job on last week's report. But I don't feel this one is up to that standard. I'd like you to have another go at it.'

Derek might not be best pleased, but he's certainly not going to feel too hard done by and he'll probably accept that the criticism is fair.

Things won't go so well if you scream at him in a shrill, hysterical voice: 'Derek – you're a lazy sod. You're a liability to this department. You look a mess as well. Your stuff is never on time, and never any good. Do this again. And this time, do it right.'

That kind of treatment is very alienating. And after it Derek is almost certainly going to regard you as the boss from hell, and he may well enlist other people to his point of view, and do everything he can to make your life difficult.

In any event, even if someone has really let you down, he or she still has rights – and those include a right to be treated with some dignity.

Giving criticism isn't easy in relationships or friendships either. But if you follow the same rules I've outlined above, it will seem less difficult.

So, if your partner isn't performing well in bed, you might gently say: 'I love it when you take your time, and stroke me gently – there.' As opposed to either saying nothing, or one day getting mad and shouting: 'Bloody hell! You're hopeless. Don't you know *anything* about love-making?'

And if you've got a flatmate – who you like and want to keep – but who never does her share of the chores, you'll certainly get much further with her if you tackle the problem assertively. For example: 'Debby, I need to talk to you. Everyone in this house has to do their share of the chores. I know it's boring, but it's a fact of life. I wonder if we could agree today on a bit of extra help from you. Could you take over the food shopping, for example?'

If you do nothing and just keep hoping the problem will go away, you'll either end up doing all the chores yourself and hating yourself because, yet again, you're allowing someone to use you as a doormat, or you'll get more and more quietly irate till you bellow at her: 'Debby! You're doing my head in. You're so selfish and lazy. Either shape up or get out.'

Now, what about *receiving* criticism? This can be very painful, but there are skills you can use to feel better about it.

For a start, when someone criticises you, *don't interrupt*!

If we interrupt, we sound rattled. We sound as if we're trying to justify ourselves against all the odds. We start over-explaining and getting more high-pitched and hysterical. We also prolong the whole process.

So if someone criticises you, bite back any response. Listen carefully. And when he or she has finished, think for a moment before you speak. Then, offer a reply. If there is any basis in the criticism, accept it and apologise. Then put your side of the argument to any part of the criticism that you know is untrue, unreasonable or unfair. Next, thank the person doing the criticising for bringing the subject into the open and giving you the chance to explain your side of the story. If there is no truth in the criticism, say: 'I'm sorry. There's no truth in that whatsoever.'

Mature, assertive people know that 'to err is human'. So they accept that they make mistakes. They are able to accept blame when it is justified and to apologise. They are also able to keep calm when they have to explain that some criticism is unjust.

So, remember to:

- be calm;
- be quietly but firmly spoken;
- keep to the point;
- use statements beginning with 'I'.

And do try not to be hard on yourself whenever you're to blame. We learn from our mistakes far more than we learn from things that we already do right. And just because you may be wrong about something, it doesn't mean you're hopeless, unlovable, stupid or bad.

Remember, we all have the right to be wrong!

Practise

If you want to be a concert pianist, you have to practise. If you want to run a marathon, you have to practise. If you want to learn to tap dance, you have to practise.

'Practice makes perfect,' our grannies used to say – and they were right. If you want to be assertive, you will also have to practise – until these skills become second nature to you.

Try using a little cassette recorder to practise asking your boss for a rise, or telling your mum not to come round this evening.

We often mentally rehearse what we're going to say in such situations, but it's much better to do it aloud. Play it back and listen to it. Hear how diffident you sound, or how you're over-explaining. Then try again. And again. Until it becomes so automatic that you won't get it wrong even if you're very nervous.

Building a good self-esteem habit is hard work but if you can polish your assertiveness skills, you will sound more effective, you will achieve much more – and you will feel 110 per cent better about yourself.

So practise, practise, practise . . . and then practise some more!

10

Deal with Your Stress: Balance Your Life

Having low self-esteem frequently causes loads of stress. You see, when you don't rate yourself as highly as you should, you tend to get stressed about lots of things. Often you also feel that you don't have the ability to sort your problems, or that you don't have a right to an easier life.

I hope that by this point in the book, you no longer believe that you're undeserving – so now is a good time to sort your stresses out properly.

Dealing with stress

Stress is important. As I described at greater length in my book *Get the Happiness Habit*, stress should be seen as a *symptom* of the fact that our lives are in some disarray, rather than as a medical condition.

Just as pain is there to alert us to the fact that something may be wrong with our physical bodies, stress is a manifestation that our mind is not in the greatest of shapes.

Ultimately, we have to eliminate the cause of the stress. But we can't always do this – not right away. Often, we have to go through periods where we are very tense and anxious but are unable, at that particular time, to sort out our reasons for feeling this way.

For example, situations such as:

- the slow death of a parent;
- a rough patch in a job where it's necessary to work evenings and weekends to save the job or company;
- knowing that your firm is making cutbacks and waiting to hear if you're going to be selected for redundancy;
- being in a bad relationship which you've decided to stick with till your kids are older;
- daily commuting – which you hate – to a job that you love or need.

For those times when we have to live with our stress – rather than be able to deal with the cause of it – we need to look at ways of reducing it.

I'm not going to go into the virtues of yoga versus circuit training here. There are more books than you can count on how to alleviate stress, and most magazines and newspapers regularly run pieces on stress-busting techniques. So, without too much trouble, you should be able to discover what the stress-busting options are, then pick one or two to help you.

However, having chosen – for example – to swim three times a week, the vital thing is to find time to do it. Any de-stressing activity – whether it's sport, massage, aromatherapy, hypnosis, relaxation tapes or meditation – is only really going to help if it's practised regularly.

Timetable your day

Apart from finding a stress buster that's going to work for you – what else can you do?

I find that the most effective way of creating calm out of chaos is to draw up a precise timetable, every day, of what you plan to achieve. Take a large sheet of paper, and then chart your day. Make a left-hand margin. In this margin, you're going to list the hours of the day: write 6 a.m., then draw a line, then write 7 a.m., and so on all the way down the page.

Next, divide the remaining width of the page into two columns. Write 'THE PLAN' as the heading of the left-hand column, and 'WHAT I ACTUALLY DID' as the heading of the right-hand one.

See the chart on p. 168. You can then draw up your daily schedule in a similar way.

Now you've got all the hours of the day and night going down the left-hand margin. Your first task is then to write down what you plan to achieve in the day, under the heading: THE PLAN.

Your second task, at the end of the day in question, is to fill in the second column – WHAT I ACTUALLY DID.

Now, one of the problems I encounter with my own clients is that they sometimes feel too stressed to even draw their chart. They say they can't find the time.

But everyone *does* have the time. So, I'd like you to decide now, when you will find time to do yours.

Basically, you're going to need to find ten minutes to do the left-hand column – THE PLAN – in the morning, or the night before.

And you're going to need to find ten minutes to fill in the right-hand column – WHAT I ACTUALLY DID – at the end of every day, or early the next morning before you forget what happened!

Decide when you can find these two slots of ten minutes each – and then stick to them.

When you begin to fill in your chart, you will probably find that your right-hand column varies quite a lot from your left-hand one. This is because you're planning too much, or too little. That is the beauty of this exercise. It shows you very clearly and very quickly what is actually happening in your day, and how it differs from what you *meant* to happen.

The purpose of this chart is to encourage you to spend your day in a balanced way. It will train you to see where you're wasting time.

TIME	THE PLAN	WHAT I ACTUALLY DID
6 a.m.		
7		
8		
9		
10		
11		
Midday		
1 p.m.		
2		
3		
4		
5		
6		
7		
8		
9		
10		
11		
Midnight		
1 a.m.		
2		
3		
4		
5		

And it will help you to discover for yourself whether or not you tend to overload your schedule.

Most people who do this plan properly over a period of several weeks find that they become calmer, and that they feel very pleased that they have actually done something to bring order and balance into their lives.

Laura

Let me tell you about Laura. She found this timetabling exercise very helpful.

Laura is a teacher. She told me she felt stressed out. And that because she couldn't get all her work done, her flat was a mess, she never had any time to get bits of shopping, and she couldn't find time to see her friends.

She started doing the daily timetable, and she discovered some useful things about herself.

She realised that she was trying to cram all her marking and her preparation for classes into the evenings, when she was tired. She was also resentful because all this work kept her from seeing friends or from getting some exercise. And the more tired and resentful she became, the harder the work seemed to be.

Also, because she was too tired and too busy to get exercise, she had decided she was getting fat. So she had been trying to eat less – and this was making her even more tired.

As for the mornings, they were very stressful because she had to drive to work in the rush hour and felt like a limp rag before the day had even started.

After a week or so of doing the daily timetable, she had completely rearranged her day. First of all, she realised that she had more energy in the mornings than the evenings. Getting up early was no problem for her, so she decided to go to school much earlier – ahead of the rush hour.

Once there, she did her marking, and her preparation of the day's classes. Soon she found that she was getting through this work more and more quickly – because she was making time for it when she felt alert.

Doing all the work early in the day released her evenings. So she was able to get out and see friends if she wanted to, and also to exercise properly.

She also realised that it was pointless cutting out food if it was making her tired and lethargic, so she decided to schedule a high-protein snack in the afternoon, after she finished work.

Before long, Laura was enjoying her teaching – and she was enjoying her life outside of school too. You can see how an average day is shaping up for her nowadays in the timetable opposite.

Step-by-step tasks

Doing a timetable chart can make a big difference in getting your day organised. But many individuals with poor self-esteem tell me that the chaos that has been building up in their lives over the years is just too big to manage. They say that when a task is huge, it is so overwhelming that they don't know where to start – and so they *don't* start.

Now, one of the problems here is that many people have a tendency to something called 'All or nothing thinking'. This means that if they can't do everything – they do nothing.

So they decide to redecorate the whole house – even if they've never picked up a paintbrush in their lives. Or they'll decide that today they'll completely clear their garage – which has got twenty years of accumulated junk in it. Or they decide to run the next London Marathon when they've taken no exercise for years.

Not surprisingly, such tasks are so onerous, they're quickly abandoned or never even begun. Don't be like this. All or nothing thinking spells DEATH to calm, practical change.

So, to tackle a big task, think one step at a time. Use the hourly timetable to re-structure your days, and when you want to make an impact on a long-term problem, like clearing out all the cupboards in the house, plan to do just fifteen minutes a day.

TIME	THE PLAN	WHAT I ACTUALLY DID
6 a.m.	Get up/shower/breakfast	Same
7	Drive to school. Have coffee. Mark homework	Same
8	Mark homework/prepare lessons	Finished all marking and preparation. Had nice chat with colleague
9	Teach	Same
10	""	""
11	""	""
Midday	Teach/lunch	Same
1 p.m.	Supervise children's lunch	Supervised kids. Also found time to pop out to local supermarket
2	Teach	Same
3	""	""
4	Drive home. Have tea, yoghurt and cheese	Same
5	Chores	Did chores quickly. Phoned friend Suzie
6	Gym	Nice evening so went running instead
7	Evening meal	Went to Suzie's for supper. Had really nice evening
8	Watch TV	Chatted with Suzie. Had 2 glasses of wine
9	Check e-mails/send e-mails	Didn't leave Suzie until 9.30. Walked home. E-mails
10	Go to bed	Pottered around. Had milky drink. Read evening paper
11	Sleep	Slept
Midnight	""	""
1 a.m.	""	""
2	""	""
3	""	""
4	""	""
5	""	""

All these fifteen-minute segments will mount up. In fact, you'll be so pleased with yourself that you'll often structure extra time to the task, and you'll get it done – one step at a time.

Balance

To have good self-esteem you have to care for yourself – all aspects of yourself. And one of the ways you can care for yourself best, is to ensure that your life is as balanced as it possibly can be.

So, if you work at a desk, you ought to get exercise in your leisure hours. If you stay at home with kids all week, then you need to have contact with adults in the evenings and at weekends. If your work is of a repetitive, practical nature, then you need to find time to stimulate your brain. If you live alone, then your leisure should include plenty of time with friends. If you commute in filthy trains and work in a polluted city, then you could do with some country air at weekends. If you're at everyone's beck and call most hours of the day, you need to find some time and space for yourself.

And, if most of your life is focused on an ambitious need to make money and be successful, then you should also find some time to feed your soul. Our souls are terribly neglected in this fast-moving world of ours, but hearing great music, looking at wonderful paintings or absorbing the architecture of an ancient cathedral – or just a solitary walk by the sea – are all ways in which we can recharge our inner needs. There are actually masses of pastimes that feed our souls, but all too frequently we decide we can't fit them into our schedules.

Often people with poor self-esteem lead a very unbalanced life. They often know this, but they decide they'll postpone sorting it until they feel more confident. Unfortunately, when you wait for improvement to just 'happen', it very rarely arrives.

So, don't wait any longer. Get moving on balancing your life – and you'll feel much better, and then your confidence and your self-esteem will improve.

Amanda

Amanda's life was very unbalanced. She worked selling advertising. The more she sold, the more money she made. She was good at the job, which was very hectic and very sociable, and she worked in a big team of equally enthusiastic, fast-living youngsters. At weekends, she went to parties and clubs. So she had a life that many people might envy – but she wasn't happy. Underneath her gregarious exterior was a very frightened woman who was terrified that her mask would slip, and that she would be revealed to be unlovable and uninteresting. These feelings, needless to say, were caused by her Negative Inner Commentary. But they were in danger of exhausting her. I've seen other people like Amanda have a complete breakdown because they weren't prepared to face their demons and sort out their lives.

Amanda was in quite a bad way. She was so anxious that if, come Wednesday, she had no social events planned for her weekend, she had a panic attack.

But, as we've already discussed, the truth is that if you're *always* expecting other people and events to 'make' you feel good, you're always going to be anxious – because other people get ill, or have to change their plans, and events sometimes get cancelled.

So, gradually, I persuaded Amanda to spend some time alone at weekends. At first she thought I was mad and was sure that this would make her feel much worse. So we started with just two hours on a Saturday afternoon when she would make her own amusement and would not see or call anyone else.

The first time she tried it, she went shopping. She didn't enjoy it much, but it wasn't too terrible either. The week after that, she went to an antique market, and the time sped by. The next week she went to an art gallery and had such a great time that the two hours became four.

Amanda still loves to party. But if there are no parties going on, she no longer thinks it's the end of the world. She now reads books. She watches the odd weepy film on TV – alone. She can also go into a coffee shop and idly read a magazine while sipping a delicious cappuccino.

She is finding time for her own being, her soul, herself. Amanda is now a much more balanced person – and her self-esteem habit has improved no end.

What we eat and drink

Balance is also important in diet. You don't need me to tell you that if you gorge on junk food and never allow a piece of fruit or a vegetable past your lips, your diet is very limited and unhealthy. Equally, if you eat nothing but fruit – and neglect carbohydrates and proteins – you're likely to feel lousy.

But even when we eat properly, we are often guilty of not drinking enough water.

Frequently, when individuals feel lethargic, muddled, sad or stressed out, they're actually dehydrated. Most of us know that we're supposed to drink eight glasses of water a day – but often we don't do it. Try to make sure that you do: your skin will benefit, and you should feel generally fitter – physically and mentally.

If you balance your life, your diet, your water intake, your spiritual needs, your family, friends and your isolation – your sense of self-worth will improve.

No one can have a very healthy self-esteem habit unless they look after themselves and their balance.

Make sure that you care for yourself

Finally, do you think that you care enough for yourself? I remember being at a party and talking to a very nice guy about a girlfriend of mine. She was lively and fun, but she was quite shy underneath and she tried to cover this up by drinking heavily. In fact she was knocking back rather too much grog as we watched and discussed her. It was obvious that the nice guy was interested in her.

'Why don't you ask her out?' I suggested.

'I would like to,' he said, 'but whenever I look at her, I just keep feeling that she's a girl who doesn't care for herself very much. And I don't want to get into all of that.'

Now, you might think that he was being unfair. And that he should have walked into her life and helped her to *learn* to care for herself. But he didn't. He just felt that someone has to care for him or herself in order to make a success of a relationship. And that having a relationship with someone who *doesn't* care for herself spells trouble.

Are you someone who looks as if you *care* for yourself? And *do* you care for yourself?

Have a think about your average day. Consult your timetable and see just how much time you spend on doing things for *you.* Does it feel like enough? If not, do something about it.

Harriet

I have a friend, Harriet, who definitely *doesn't* care enough for herself. She's got a very exacting job and three children, and a husband who's a poorly paid artist and pretty temperamental into the bargain.

Harriet loves her man. And she's committed to the marriage. But she looks stressed out. Why? Because her whole life is spent sorting her husband, the children – and working to keep them all. She confided to me that she had dropped all her friends, because there was no time to see them. And yet, as she very well knew, they would have given her the support and care that she needed. She insists that there's absolutely nothing she can do right now to change her life for the better. She feels she just has to put up with it.

Are you like Harriet? I hope not. So, draw up a list of things that you know would change it for the better – things that would be good for *you*, and would show that you *care* for you.

They may be big tasks like taking a degree at the Open University. Or they may be simple, like having a cup of coffee once a week with an old girlfriend.

Whatever they are, take steps to incorporate them into your life.

Care for yourself, and you'll feel much better about yourself. And other people will feel better about you too.

11

Keeping Up Your Self-Esteem in Difficult Relationships

People with poor self-esteem often say that they find it hard to get into a good relationship.

This is true. What's *also* true is that people with poor self-esteem find it even harder to get out of bad ones.

So far in this book, I've tried to encourage you to the view that you are vital, special, lovely and viable – whether or not you're in a relationship.

I have also spent some time in trying to help readers who find it difficult to meet new people – and therefore to get into relationships – to overcome their diffidence, and break out of their old way of doing things.

Many individuals with poor self-esteem are, however, already *in* relationships. But a substantial number of those individuals are in unhealthy relationships which cause them much misery – and they often stay in those relationships, because they honestly believe that *anything* is better than being single. This is nonsense of course, and it's rarely a good enough reason for staying put.

People who have insufficient self-esteem find the thought of being alone absolutely terrifying. So, because they're frightened, and because they don't think they deserve very much in life, they put up with treatment from their partners that is demeaning and unsupportive and unloving. And they don't seem to be able to see a way out of it. In fact, they often get to the stage where they have no idea of what is normal in a relationship – and what's not.

What's normal and what's not

Often, people with poor self-esteem are so blinded by their own faults that they don't consider their partner has any. They are also, as I've just said, so desperate to keep the relationship going at all costs that they put up with anything.

So, let me just run through some common relationship situations that people with poor self-esteem put up with – and try to identify whether or not they are normal.

Violence – physical and verbal

There is never, ever, *ever* any excuse for physical violence in a relationship. This applies just as much to women hitting men as it does to men hitting women. Having said that, *most* women with violent tendencies do not hurt men very much, as men are generally stronger. But it is very isolating being a man who gets hit – because society as a whole dismisses this, or seems to think it's funny. And of course it is just as degrading for a man to be physically attacked as it is for a woman.

The fact is, however, that far more women than men are on the receiving end of physical violence. And most men have no concept at all of just how terrifying it is to a woman to be overpowered by a male.

But an equal and loving relationship should never include violence: physical violence in a relationship is NOT normal.

It is also not normal to be in a relationship where there is verbal abuse. Of course, everyone gets cross from time to time, but it is quite unacceptable to be told: 'you're fat, you're useless, you're stupid, you're not sexy' – or anything else that strikes at the very heart of who and what you are.

It is also unacceptable to be constantly sworn at. 'You fucking bitch', for example, is not a form of address that is appropriate.

Sometimes, adults with little self-regard are so used to being insulted that they don't realise it's happening. But if this is part of your relationship, it's time to summon the courage to say, 'Please don't talk to me like that ever again.'

And if it doesn't stop, ask yourself why you're in this relationship. And if your only answer is that you're terrified of being on your own, then re-double your efforts to challenge your Negative Inner Commentary. Also start making practical plans for a time when you feel ready to walk away from a situation that is undoubtedly damaging you.

Compromise

When a relationship isn't going too well, people often ask me how much compromise they should be prepared to make.

The truth is that there's no relationship – not even the most magical, romantic, passionate, loving or companionable relationship in the world – that doesn't require compromise from time to time. But there should be an appropriate balance.

So, if your partner has PMS for a week each month and is argumentative and unreasonable, you may have to compromise by putting up with this – because the rest of the time, everything's great. This will be a workable arrangement, so long as she is particularly loving and reasonable at other times to make up for the week when she's not.

Similarly, perhaps your husband is studying for important exams – and in order to help him, you're paying for everything, as well as doing all the chores in the house. Clearly, this isn't a very balanced existence and you're putting up with an awful lot. But it can be seen as an acceptable, temporary compromise so long as he shows you how grateful he is in words and actions – and also so long as he shoulders at least half of these responsibilities after his exams are over.

It's important to work out compromises about other, rather more commonplace, situations that tend to cause trouble. For example, there's the vexed question of which set of parents you're going to visit at Christmas. If you feel hard done by because every year you go to your partner's parents for the festive season – and you hate it because you don't feel at home and the kids have to share your room and you feel too inhibited to have sex – then obviously Christmas is not a bundle of laughs for you!

You might agree to this arrangement on alternate years – but to do it every year suggests you're being railroaded into submission. And if there's too much take and not enough give from your partner in other areas of the relationship too, then it's time to stand up calmly but firmly for more equality.

There are other – seemingly silly – compromises in most relationships. One of you may like to read or listen to the radio in bed, and may find it impossible to sleep unless you can wind down in this way. The other partner may prefer to go straight to sleep and may well find the radio and light a nuisance. Well obviously there are practical solutions here. The wakeful one can read or listen to the radio in another room (though I don't advocate this, as it doesn't do much for the closeness of the relationship). Or he or she can wear a personal set of headphones, and the sleepy one can wear an eyeshade.

This is a normal sort of compromise situation between two people who are in an equal relationship. But if there are a lot of similar situations which all favour one person – then the situation is not normal.

Often, when someone has poor self-esteem they 'compromise' all the time – to the extent that they become a doormat which constantly gets trodden on. Let me tell you a little story:

A young actress was working all summer in a weekly Repertory Company. This is a marvellous way to learn your craft, but it's tough. It means that you're reading through one play, learning another, and actually acting in another – all at the same time.

You rehearse all day, and then you act in the evening. And after this – and maybe a quick visit to the pub to keep you sane – you go back to your 'digs' to learn a whole chunk of next week's play. You have to do this because you're going to need to know it for the rehearsal next morning.

This young actress was living with her boyfriend, who was also going through the same rigorous schedule. But he maintained that it was harder for him to learn his script.

So, every night after they finished acting, they went back to their lodgings – and she sat up with him helping him to learn his part. Eventually, after a couple of hours or so, he would be satisfied that he knew enough, and would turn the light off and go to sleep.

And what did she do?

Well, she would go next door to the bathroom and sit on the loo and learn her own script – well into the wee small hours. In fact it was often daylight before she had finished.

Do you think this was a very equal relationship? No? No, neither do I. But I was that young actress – and at the time I wasn't ready to see that I wasn't standing up for my own rights. I thought that I had to put up with being treated that way, because I didn't deserve any better and also that I wouldn't get another bloke if I walked away from that one.

So, you see, I do know what it's like to be in such a situation, and to have such skewed thinking – and it's miserable.

Are you making the same sorts of mistakes in your relationship? If so, how many situations are there in your relationship where you put up with things that you're not happy with? Make a list. If it's a long list, this should tell you that it's time to do something about it.

Sex as a punishment

Some individuals withhold sex and closeness as a form of punishment. Others inflict and impose sex as a form of punishment. Neither is a normal state of affairs.

A friend of mine, Fiona, has always had plenty of confidence workwise, but is very uncertain of herself in romantic situations.

Time after time, she's picked the wrong guy: the sort of bloke who made her self-esteem worse, not better. Her lowest ebb came when she was living with an alcoholic who used to withhold sex for a punishment.

Thankfully, after a while, she plucked up the courage to face up to how things were – and she did begin to question what on earth she was doing with a man who could be so weird and so unkind to her. She took herself off for some therapy. Later, she dumped the alcoholic, and she's now in love with someone who thinks she's wonderful – and treats her as such.

It is remarkably easy for anyone to believe that what goes on in their house and in their bed is normal – when nothing could be farther from the truth. Withholding sex and warmth as a punishment is cruel, and never justified. And it also goes without saying that forcing someone into having sex is also totally unacceptable. So, if either of these things is happening to you, please have a think about your rights as a human being. You deserve better: much better. What you're putting up with is not normal.

Partners who are unavailable

It's an unfortunate fact that many people who have poor self-regard pick lousy partners for themselves. These partners may be unsuitable, or unkind, but frequently they are just not fully available in some way or another.

I have a distant cousin who is attractive, warm and intelligent. She has a good job as a university lecturer, but she *always* gets saddled with the wrong man.

There was one who was into S and M and who didn't want a long-term *normal* sexual relationship. There was one who was married. Another one didn't want to upset a past 'sensitive' girlfriend by getting properly involved with anyone else. Then there was the bloke who later came out as gay. And there was yet another who was so puritanical that he only fancied sex about twice a year.

It is not normal to put up with these situations. And it's definitely not normal if you keep repeating the pattern.

So, if you're a bit accident-prone when it comes to relationships, make yourself a list of what went wrong with each of them: the chances are that the same thing goes wrong every time – in some form or another.

If this is so, it will help you greatly to see that you are doing all of this to yourself. These situations are not just *happening* to you – but at some level, you are *causing* them to happen.

If we look very carefully at relationships that apparently go wrong, we often find that the honest truth is that they were never right in the first place! And that's certainly true of my cousin. So why would someone classy and special keep starting relationships that are never going to go anywhere? Have a think about this – especially if it applies personally to you. Ninety-nine times out of a hundred, it's because of an absence of a good self-esteem habit.

So try to remember: you deserve to have a normal, loving relationship. If you keep picking the wrong partners, persevere at improving your self-esteem habit and you'll find you stop doing it.

Affairs

Of course the classic case of a partner not being fully available is when he or she is living with someone else – in other words, when your relationship is an 'affair'.

Now, it would be untrue to say that affairs always end unhappily (although it *would* be true to say that virtually every affair is painful to *someone*). Many couples who are in a very happy second marriage started their romance as an affair – and for them it certainly worked out well. But compared to other affairs, these situations are in the minority.

Many people with poor self-esteem find themselves in a relationship-triangle. They never saw themselves as being likely to end up in a clandestine romance, but somehow it happened. Often it 'happens' time and time again.

Having poor self-esteem makes it likely that you'll put up with being a kind of 'reserve' in love – and that is only going to damage you further.

I'm always getting letters from adults who say that they've spent years and years as a secret lover – and that they've never been put first, and never been able to guarantee that they could spend Christmas or birthdays with the person they love most in the world.

Frequently, their married lover lies to them, saying that when his or her kids grow up all will be well. But the fact is that if a married person doesn't leave home for a lover within the first year of starting another relationship, then it's unlikely to ever happen. And many adults – usually men – who do leave home after their kids have flown the nest, don't settle with the long-term lover who's comforted them through the years: they find someone new.

So, if you're in an affair with someone who lives with someone else, have a care. It may mean that you'll give up your own chance of being a parent, and that you'll live a lie for years and never have anything concrete to show for it. This kind of situation is likely to increase your feelings of being undeserving and worthless. So, as you keep working at this book, just keep asking yourself:

- Is this affair good for me?
- Is it helping me to have a fulfilled, happy, balanced life?
- Would I sooner be *in* this affair than *out* of it?

I think you'll find that, as your habit of self-esteem grows, it will be harder and harder to answer 'yes' to any of these three questions.

Lots of people have affairs. Maybe some are harmless and fun – but I don't tend to hear about those. However, waiting around for someone who never delivers what they promise is degrading – and it certainly can't be classed as normality.

Porn and the Internet

There are obviously many women who enjoy a bit of pornography for personal sexual relief. There are others who like to watch an occasional raunchy video, or read an explicit book with their lovers – as part of their menu of love.

So far, however, I have never heard of a heterosexual relationship that was foundering because of a woman's porn habit. I do, on the other hand, get masses of e-mails – and I also hear of all sorts of difficulties from my own clients – about men who seem to have a growing dependence on top-shelf magazines, saucy videos, and, most commonly of all nowadays, porn on the Internet.

Now, if you are a woman with poor self-regard – especially if you could be keener on your own body – the porn thing may be a big issue for you. But what you may find it difficult to ascertain is what's normal and what's not.

Let me try and help. I'll begin by explaining about male masturbation. Most men with a normal sex drive will masturbate from time to time even if they are in a loving long-term relationship. It always amazes me that some women in these modern times are surprised, shocked or disgusted by this fact, but it happens to be the truth. And many of these men use pictures or video images to increase their pleasure in solo sex. This is normal behaviour.

So, it's not surprising that many men have found porn on the Internet and have had a good look at it, and have masturbated to various images that they've found there. (Frankly, I don't find the idea of touching oneself up sitting by a computer screen the least bit sexy – but it's clear that plenty of people do.) And in the twenty-first century, this too could be construed as normal.

However, a growing number of women complain that their partners seem less and less interested in normal sex and prefer the Internet. Many of them tell me how they go to bed, hoping their partner will follow – but instead he stays up, accessing porn on the computer.

Not surprisingly, plenty of adult women find this insulting. They also feel undermined because they believe that all the females on the Net have flawless figures, quite forgetting that many of their bodies have been surgically enhanced, as well as filmed from the most flattering angles.

Women whose husbands and partners are into Internet porn can also feel frustrated because their own sexual needs aren't being catered for. And of course if they already have feelings of being undeserving, worthless, unlovable, unattractive or unwanted, then their man's porn habit is likely to increase these feelings.

My view is that if a bloke is spending more and more time on Internet sex, and less and less time with his partner, then this is *not* normal and he has a problem.

So, if by chance you are in this situation with a partner, and when you try to talk to him about it he fobs you off by saying that you're 'hysterical' or 'out of date' or 'puritanical' – don't believe him. His behaviour is not normal and there's no reason why you should put up with it.

Incidentally, some men with an Internet porn habit actually have very real difficulties with relationships. A lot of them also have specific sexual problems such as premature ejaculation (this means that they 'come' too quickly), or ejaculatory incompetence (which means they find it difficult or impossible to ejaculate into a vagina).

If your partner is one of these men, try to get him to see that he needs help. (There are details of psychosexual therapy in the Help Yourself Guide at the end of the book.)

If he can't – or won't – see that his habit is out of control, please ask yourself whether you are prepared to play second best to two-dimensional air-brushed fantasy figures, when your man could be enjoying the reality of your warm and loving body in the comfort of a cosy bed.

As you work on your Negative Inner Commentaries, and on being in touch with your own goodness and kindness, you'll find you are less and less likely to accept that your treatment at the hands of a porn-addicted partner is something you should put up with.

Poor self-esteem can make *you* behave badly

So far in this chapter, we've looked at problematic relationships where the person with poor self-esteem is being treated badly by a partner.

But sometimes, it's the person with the poor self-esteem who behaves badly. As I said earlier in Chapter One, most people imagine that someone with poor self-esteem is always quiet, inhibited and shy. But this isn't always the case. There are actually some individuals with a very poor sense of their own value who seem outgoing and bubbly and apparently assertive – even aggressive.

Recently, I met a number of women who fit this kind of profile when I was working on ITV's *Trisha* series.

For those of you who're never at home in the mornings, this is a programme where people talk about their relationship difficulties in front of a studio audience, and a television audience of millions.

Many of these adults are very damaged and sad. But they've tried to cope with these feelings by being feisty and loud – and by making huge demands of their partners.

One woman recently was so afraid that her husband would leave her – and was so jealous if he so much as looked at another woman – that she wouldn't let him go out alone, banned all newspapers from the house, and stopped him from watching television.

When I got up close to this young wife, it was clear that she was really panic-stricken – and that her rating of herself and her body was practically zero. But she covered all this up by being aggressive and demanding.

I doubt very much if anyone reading this book is in quite that bad a state, but if you know that you deal with your lack of self-esteem by being very argumentative in your relationship, I urge you to:

- keep working at changing your NICs into PICs;
- keep trying to get in touch with your own goodness;
- pay particular attention to Chapter Nine and learn how to be assertive without being aggressive;
- remember that in any relationship you don't need to win every battle.

This last point is very important. Frequently, people who don't value themselves will refuse to let a subject drop, even when it would be much wiser to do so.

In any relationship, there are going to be differences of opinion, but sometimes it's better to just accept that you can't possibly see eye to eye about everything.

So, when some difference of opinion is eating away at you, even though it's been discussed thoroughly, don't go on and on about it. This will only irritate your partner more and is unlikely to help you win the argument.

Instead, make a note of the problem and how you feel about it, and then close the notebook and leave it alone for a couple of days. Often when this happens, you find that the whole issue isn't such a big deal after all. But if you still feel misunderstood, then arrange a time with your partner when you will discuss it again.

I do try not to latch on to gender stereotypes, but it is true to say that often men and women have completely different views about how much a difficulty gets discussed.

A man may say: 'We go over this time and time again.' While his partner may say: 'We never discuss it.'

They can't both be right! It just shows that on the whole men and women approach problems differently.

So it makes sense when there are lots of arguments and differences of opinion to adopt the 'ten-minute rule'. This means that you both agree to discuss something properly – without either of you swearing, or leaving the room, slamming doors etc. – for ten minutes each. You should get a clock and put it down on the table and then toss a coin to see which of you should have your say first.

Ten minutes can seem like an age to a guy who doesn't want to get into all of this, but it can seem like no time at all to a woman determined to make her point. So the procedure is a good exercise in compromise for both parties! And the fact that there is a definite time limit means that the whole situation shouldn't get out of hand.

One of you gives his or her point of view for ten minutes while the other listens and doesn't interrupt. Then the other speaks for ten minutes. At the end of that time, hopefully each of you will understand the other better, even if you can't still fully agree. It's important then to leave the subject.

In a relationship where there are lots of arguments, the ten-minute rule can work wonders. It's also a good idea to agree that you will never quarrel after nine o'clock at night, because there's a strong possibility that you're both tired, and that at least one of you may have had an alcoholic drink or two. So if you start to get cross with each other, agree that you will put the whole problem on ice till a more suitable time.

Time to get out

Several times during this chapter, I have suggested that you should consider leaving a relationship if it is damaging you.

This is a very difficult concept for many people to deal with, especially if the relationship – flawed though it may be – spells the only security that they have known. It's also difficult to leave a relationship if you have young children at home.

But if you work on your self-esteem, your relationship may well improve. And if it doesn't, you'll begin to feel stronger within yourself and you'll find a way to get out of what previously seemed like an impossible situation.

Some people who have arrived at the belief that they must end a relationship – but who feel they must stay till their children are older – decide to begin planning now for a time when they can be on their own.

They make a kind of pact with themselves, and they start quietly working towards a new life. This sort of 'project' is very good at increasing a person's self-value.

If you are such a person, for a start, you might confide in a friend and tell that person your plans. You might open a separate bank account. You might talk to the Citizens' Advice Bureau about your legal rights. And you might decide to take some qualifications or embark on some re-training so that you'll be ready for a new career when you emerge from the relationship.

This kind of planning is a good compromise in difficult situations and it puts you firmly in the driving seat – which is a good place to be if you want to enhance your self-esteem.

Finally, I came across this quote the other day by the American writer, Maureen Dowd. It might help you to remember it:

'The minute you settle for less than you deserve, you get even less than you settled for.'

12

Maintaining Your New, Good Habit

Congratulations for travelling with me thus far. But where do you go from here?

The important thing is to go forward with everything you've learned, and to take life by the scruff of the neck.

You've learned ways to challenge your damaging thoughts. And you've also learned many practical skills that will help you feel and appear more confident.

And now all you have to do is to practise what you've learned for the rest of your life!

Just remember that:

- you are unique;
- you are special;
- you are likeable;
- you are lovable;
- you are worthwhile;
- you deserve love;
- you have the right to be happy;
- others have the right to be happy;

- you have the right to make mistakes;
- others have the right to make mistakes;
- you are ultimately responsible for how you live your life;
- you *can* change, and you can achieve a fulfilled, contented life.

At this point in the book, it would be a great idea to go back and re-do all the tests in Chapter Two.

You might also like to check on the original goals in Chapter One. You see, you may feel that you've still got a long way to go in order to achieve a great self-esteem habit, but I bet you've come further than you think – and looking back at the early chapters will confirm that for you.

Finally, let me ask you the question that I started with: *Are you your own favourite person?*

I do so hope that you are.

The Help Yourself Guide

This last chapter is designed to provide you with extra help that you might need in order to sustain and improve your self-esteem habit. It includes details of useful support groups, sound tapes and books.

Therapy

Having got to the end of this book, you may decide that you could do with extra help in your quest for a good self-esteem habit. So you may feel that the time has come to get some one-to-one therapy.

But making this decision is just the start! The next step can be quite bewildering. Where to begin? What are the different types of therapy? How much is it all going to cost? How should you select your therapist?

Here's my brief summary of the complex world of counselling and psychotherapy, which I hope will lead you to find the right practitioner for you.

What's available on the NHS?

Much depends on where you live, how old you are, and whether your GP has a resident counsellor attached to his or her practice. The best thing to do is to ask your GP what's available.

Family Planning Clinics counsel people on sexual matters, free of charge. So do Genito-Urinary Medicine Clinics. And so do psychosexual units in some large NHS hospitals, but to be seen in one of these, you need a referral from your GP.

Other low cost or free counselling

For readers under twenty-five, there is a network of Brook Centres for Young People. They counsel on contraception, various sexual problems and relationships. Call their central helpline: 08000 185023 for more information.

Also for younger people, counselling is often available free from colleges and university services, and from local authorities.

There is also Youth Access which is an organisation providing free counselling nationwide on all sorts of matters. Call: 020 8772 9900.

Some psychotherapy organisations offer low-cost therapy from their trainees. Obviously this sort of practitioner will not be vastly experienced, but he or she will probably be very keen – and will be thoroughly supervised by an expert. (There's a list of professional organisations later in the chapter.)

Relate – formerly Marriage Guidance – offers relationship counselling for couples or individuals, whether they're straight or gay. Fees are calculated according to a client's means. Tel: 01788 573241.

In Scotland, the equivalent organisation is Couples Counselling Scotland. Tel: 0131 556 1527.

CRUSE, which is the national organisation for bereaved people, offers free telephone counselling. There are also local groups. Ring their helpline on: 0870 167 1677.

Private psychotherapy/counselling – and who offers it

Many people wonder if there is a difference between psychotherapy and counselling. There used to be, but nowadays the two terms are virtually interchangeable.

As well as psychotherapists and counsellors, many psychiatrists offer psychotherapy in the private sector. A psychiatrist is a medical doctor who has gone on to specialise in mental health. Not all psychiatrists are skilled in psychotherapy. Many are more concerned with medication.

There are also psychologists. A psychologist is not a medical doctor. Instead, he or she has a degree in psychology. But there are all sorts of psychologists. Many of them are academics who never come into contact with real patients. A psychologist who sees patients/clients is generally called a clinical psychologist, or a chartered psychologist.

A major difference between a psychiatrist and all the other practitioners is that psychiatrists, being medical doctors, can prescribe drugs while the others can't.

Qualifications

Clearly a psychiatrist will have a string of medical qualifications attached to his or her name. And a psychologist will have a degree – and probably other professional qualifications too. But when it comes to counsellors and psychotherapists the picture is less clear.

At present, there's no legal requirement for a therapist to have passed any exams, or to have trained properly, or to belong to a professional organisation. Obviously this means that there are some dodgy therapists about. So do pick someone who is a member of one of the professional organisations which I've listed later in this chapter.

Different types of therapy

Once you have decided which type of practitioner you want to see, you still have to decide what sort of therapy would best suit you.

Behaviour Therapy

If you have a phobia – including a social phobia where you feel anxious about blushing, or public speaking, or eating in public – Behaviour Therapy can be most helpful.

It won't concern itself much with your thinking, but will simply address how your problem affects your behaviour and causes difficulties for you. There is much emphasis on good breathing and distraction techniques, and on facing up to tasks that have always been difficult.

This is an active, collaborative, short-term and skills-enhancing therapy.

Cognitive Therapy (frequently practised in conjunction with Behaviour Therapy, and then called Cognitive Behaviour Therapy, or CBT)

The main thrust of Cognitive Therapy is that our thoughts create our moods. During the course of treatment, we learn that we all have inherent tendencies to certain negative thoughts that evoke unhappiness and disturbance. Once we accept this fact, we can learn to spot our negative thoughts as they arise, and then challenge and re-think them.

You will probably realise that many of the ideas in this book are based on the principles of CBT.

The results of Cognitive Therapy have been well researched. In the treatment of depression, for example, it has been found to be more helpful than any other kind of treatment, including anti-depressants, for significant numbers of individuals.

CT or CBT is particularly well suited to helping people with poor self-esteem.

Eclectic or Integrative Therapy

Eclectic or integrative practitioners don't adhere rigidly to any particular therapeutic model. Instead, they use techniques from many different schools of thought – according to the needs of individual clients. It can be most helpful in the hands of an expert who will custom-build your treatment to suit you.

Gestalt Therapy

This is a therapy that is concerned with a holistic view of human beings. It places great emphasis on trusting our own thoughts and our own bodies.

Gestalt Therapy seems to be particularly effective for rather 'buttoned-up' individuals because it seeks to open up past, relevant emotions and relate them to the present.

It can be a very emotional experience, and if you're considering it, you should make sure you're going to someone who's experienced enough to handle all your pent-up feelings.

Person-centred Therapy (PCT)

A person-centred therapist's attitude to the client is one of total acceptance of the client as he or she is at present – not simply of how the person might become.

At the heart of the therapy is the belief that if a person is cared for (even if just by the therapist) then that person begins to feel – at quite a deep level – that he or she is *worth* caring for.

This kind of therapy is good for clients who denigrate themselves and who have poor self-esteem.

PCT encourages them to give up all their developed notions of how they *should* be, and to find and accept their real selves. It also encourages a greater understanding of other people.

Psychodynamic Therapy

This is a generic term that embraces all therapies of an *analytic* nature. Probably the majority of psychodynamicists adhere to the teaching of Freud. But there are also Jungian and Adlerian therapists.

In this type of therapy, the therapist keeps his own personality and all details about himself right out of the picture. In fact, the practitioner is like a blank canvas on to which the patient can transfer and project deep feelings about himself, his parents, and other significant players in his life. It is then up to the therapist to handle all the feelings and information which emerge: and gradually to help the patient to deal with all this 'baggage' and thus gain a better understanding of what his disturbances are, and how his mind works.

This is a long-term therapy – which often takes place at least twice a week for several years.

You are not likely to be attracted by this therapeutic approach unless you are interested in examining your past in detail. You should also have lots of time and money. Don't pick a psychodynamic therapist if you're looking for down to earth and pragmatic advice.

Questions to ask when you phone a therapist

When you decide to go for therapy, you'll probably select two or three possible therapists from various sources – and then you'll phone up to find out more.

Make a list of what you want to ask, as you may be feeling nervous. You may want to know very practical things such as:

- Is the practice on a bus route?
- Is there car parking space?
- Is there a waiting room? (Some therapists work in such tiny premises that there isn't one, which means you're a bit stuck if you've come by public transport and you turn up early. You might

end up standing out in the street till the therapist has finished with his previous client!)

- Is there a loo you can use? (Many clients feel very nervous about therapy and like to know there is a lavatory for their use on the premises.)

If you're happy with the practical arrangements you should discuss the problems you want to get help with. You then need to ask:

- Do you belong to any particular therapeutic school of thought? (Obviously you may already know this if you have selected someone from an organisation that makes it clear what type of therapy is on offer.)
- What are your qualifications – and which professional organisations do you belong to?
- How often are the sessions? (Most therapists will expect you to come weekly at first – but psychodynamic therapists frequently ask new clients to come more regularly.)
- How much does each session cost?
- What are the arrangements for cancelling a session? Is there a cancellation charge?
- How long – roughly – will I be in therapy?
- Have you got any specific experience of helping my type of problem?
- Can I smoke in the consulting room?

After this kind of preliminary conversation, you might want to take a day or two to think about what you've learned from the phone call. I urge you NOT to book an appointment, unless you feel comfortable talking to that particular person.

There are a great number of therapists, so don't book up with the first one you try unless you feel you really like the sound of him or her.

Fees (at the time of publication)

Fees for professional private therapy vary enormously. You're unlikely to find anything costing less than £25 per hour, and you might encounter much larger fees. Top psychiatrists or psychologists in Harley Street, for example, tend to charge between £90 and £150 per hour.

Most people – depending on where they live in the country – should be able to find therapy from a properly qualified practitioner for around £40 to £50 per hour.

Professional organisations

In some ways, finding a therapist is easier today than it was a couple of years ago, as so many of the reputable organisations now have websites – and on most of these sites you can actually find a list of therapists in your area.

These organisations are also useful if you ever have any complaint to make about one of their therapists – or if you're ever having doubts about the methods used in your treatment.

- United Kingdom Council for Psychotherapy – this is an umbrella organisation for many different psychotherapeutic groups and is a great place to find a therapist. Tel: 020 7436 3002. Web address: www.psychotherapy.org.uk.
- British Association for Counselling and Psychotherapy. Tel: 0870 4435252.
- British Psychological Society. Tel: 0116 2549568. Web address: www.bps.org.uk.
- Royal College of Psychiatrists. Tel: 020 7235 2351. Web address: www.rcpsych.ac.uk.
- National Council of Psychotherapists – established in 1971 and representing the practice of psychotherapy on a fully eclectic basis. Tel: 0115 913 1382. Web address: www.natcouncilofpsychotherapists.org.uk.

- British Association of Psychotherapists – the members of this association are psychodynamic therapists of the Freudian or Jungian type. Tel: 020 8452 9823. Web address: www.bap-psycho therapy.org.
- British Association for Behavioural and Cognitive Psychotherapies – this organisation will help you to find a properly qualified cognitive therapist, cognitive behaviour therapist, or behaviour therapist. Tel: 01254 875277. Web address: www.babcp.org.
- Gestalt Centre. Tel: 020 7613 4480. Web address: www.gestalt centre.co.uk. Also, The Gestalt Therapy Page (www.gestalt.org) gives details of Gestalt therapists worldwide.
- National Council For Hypnotherapy. Many practitioners who practise hypnosis also offer counselling or psychotherapy, usually of an integrated nature. Hypnosis can help with coming to terms with past events and is a useful tool for relaxation. Tel: 0800 9520545. Web address: www.hypnotherapists.org.uk.

Assertiveness

You may not want psychotherapy or counselling, but you may decide that you could do with some more assertiveness skills.

Nowadays, it's relatively easy to get this kind of help. Virtually every adult education authority runs assertiveness classes as part of its programme of events for adult learners. You can find out what's available in your area from your public library, or from the adult education department of your local council.

The Industrial Society also runs excellent courses in assertiveness. For further details, ring them on: 0870 400 1000.

Further reading

An A–Z Guide to Drug-Free Health by Maryon and Alan Stewart. Vermilion, price £12.99.

Anorexia Nervosa by Janet Treasure. Psychology Press, price £9.99.

Be Your Own Life Coach by Fiona Harrold. Hodder and Stoughton, price £10.00.

Breaking Free – Help for Survivors of Child Sexual Abuse by Carolyn Ainscough and Kay Toon. Sheldon Press, price £10.99.

Bulimia Nervosa and Binge-Eating by Peter J. Cooper. Robinson, price £6.99.

Confidence Works – Learn to Be Your Own Life Coach by Gladeana McMahon. Sheldon Press, price £7.99.

Cope With Your Biological Clock by Theresa Francis-Cheung. Hodder and Stoughton, price £6.99.

Find the Love Of Your Life by Julia Cole. Hodder and Stoughton, price £6.99.

Get Everything Done by Mark Forster. Hodder and Stoughton, price £6.99.

Get the Happiness Habit by Christine Webber. Hodder and Stoughton, price £6.99.

Life Coaching – Change Your Life in 7 Days, by Eileen Mulligan. Piatkus, price £8.99.

Loving Yourself Loving Another by Julia Cole. Vermilion, price £7.99.

Mind Over Mood by Dennis Greenberger and Christine Padesky. Guilford Press, price £16.00.

Overcoming Anorexia Nervosa by Christopher Freeman. Robinson, price £7.99.

Overcoming Childhood Trauma by Helen Kennerley. Robinson, price £7.99.

Overcoming Social Anxiety and Shyness by Gillian Butler. Robinson, price £7.99.

Support groups

Acne Support Group – real understanding and up to date medical advice for this most distressing condition. Tel: 020 8841 4747. Web address: www.m2w3.com/acne.

Eating Disorders Association. Tel: 01603 621414. Web address: www.edauk.com.

Families Need Fathers – a group for men whose relationship difficulties have led to problems in maintaining contact with their children. Tel: 020 7613 5060.

National Phobics Society – a group run by sufferers and ex-sufferers of phobias, social anxiety, OCD, panic attacks, and other stress-related conditions. Tel: 0870 7700456. Web address: www.phobics-society.org.uk.

PACS (Post-Abortion Counselling Service). Tel: 020 7221 9631.

Samaritans – a listening ear for distressed, depressed and suicidal people, 24 hours a day, 365 days a year. Tel: 08457 909090.

Sex Addicts Anonymous. Tel: 020 8946 2436.

SPOD – the association to aid the sexual and personal relationships of people with a disability. Tel: 020 7607 8851. Web address: www.spod-uk.org.

Survivors – this is a support group for male survivors of childhood sexual abuse and rape. Tel: 020 7357 6677. Web address: www.survivorsuk.org.uk.

Women's Aid National Helpline – a helpline for women in jeopardy from physical, verbal and mental violence. Tel: 08457 023468.

Useful websites

Lifeskills – run by an eminent behavioural psychologist, this is a site where you can buy sound tapes to help you with a range of problems including insomnia and shyness – www.lifeskills.gg.

Loot Personals – a well-regulated, legal, honest and truthful site for finding friends or romance – www.loot.com.

Match.com – is one of the leading global Internet dating services – www.match.com.

On Divorce – everything you need to know about the practical and emotional issues surrounding divorce – www.ondivorce.co.uk.

Single Again – a website run by an organisation for people who have returned to being single after having been in a relationship: advice on how to have a life even though you may not currently have a partner – www.singleagain.co.uk.

Index